The Blackstone Franks Good Investment Guide

The Blackstone Franks Good Investment Guide

An A-Z for Personal Investors

Kogan Page

First published in Great Britain by
Kogan Page Limited 1987
120 Pentonville Road, London N1 9JN

British Library Cataloguing in Publication Data
Blackstone Franks
The Blackstone Franks good investment guide.
1. Investments—Great Britain
I. Title
332.6'0941 HG5432

ISBN 1-85091-356-0

Printed and bound in Great Britain by
Biddles Ltd, Guildford
Surrey.

CONTENTS

Introduction	1
The Blackstone Franks rating system	3
'Angel' investments	7
Annuities	8
Annuities to secure endowment policies ('Back to back' arrangements)	10
Antiques	11
Bank deposits	13
Building societies	14
Business expansion schemes (BES)	15
Busted bonds	17
Capital conversion schemes	19
Capital gift plan	19
Certificates of tax deposit	20
Commodities	21
Deeds of covenant	23
Diamonds	24
Endowment policies	25
Equity linked savings plans (*see* Unit-linked savings plans)	31
Extra interest accounts	31
Farms	33
Friendly societies	33
Gilt conversion plans (*see* Capital conversion schemes)	35
Gilts	35
Gold	39
Granny bonds	39
Guaranteed income bonds	39
Holiday lettings	41
Home – your own	42
Home income plans	42
Hospital insurance	44
Income and growth bonds	45
Index-linked investments	45
Investment bonds	46
Investment trusts	50
Krugerrands	55
Leasing equipment	57
Life assurance	57

Contents

Limited editions	58
Lloyd's underwriters	58
Local authority loans	61
Local authority stocks or bonds	61
Managed or mixed funds	63
Maximum investment plans	63
Money market	63
National savings	65
National savings certificates	66
National savings deposit bonds	67
National savings investment accounts	67
Offshore funds	69
Options	70
Over the counter market	72
Pensions – company schemes	73
Pensions – self-administered schemes	76
Pensions – self-employed	77
Permanent health insurance (PHI)	78
Personal accident and sickness insurance	80
Personal equity plans (PEP)	81
Premium bonds	89
Prime residential property funds	89
Private medical plans	90
Property investment	92
Quoted securities (*see* Stock Exchange)	95
Racehorses	97
Retirement annuities (*see* pensions – self-employed)	97
School fees planning	99
Second homes	102
Shares (*see* Stock Exchange)	102
Share option schemes (approved)	103
Single premium bonds (*see* Investment bonds)	105
Stamps	105
Stock Exchange	106
Term life assurance	109
Trusts	111
Trusts – accumulation and maintenance trusts	114
Umbrella funds	115

Unit-linked life assurance	116
Unit-linked savings plans	116
Unit trusts	117
Unlisted securities market	121
War loan (*see* Gilts)	123
Whole life assurance	123
Wills	124
Wine	126
Woodlands	126
Zero coupon bonds	127

The Authors

Bill Blevins, CII AII, was Senior Inspector and Trusts and Taxation specialist at Norwich Union until 1981. He was in charge of Technical Services at Canada Life until March 1984 when he joined Blackstone Franks as Managing Director. Bill Blevins lectures on investment planning and is a member of the Chartered Insurance Institute, the Institute of Taxation and the British Institute of Management.

Lance R Blackstone, B Comm FCA, became a manager with Manufacturers Hanover Ltd and left in 1975 to go into private practice as an accountant. He writes and lectures widely on taxation, business and investments.

David S Franks, B Comm MBA FCA, worked for Chase Manhattan Bank in London and New York in domestic and international financing until 1975 when he entered private practice. He writes and lectures widely on taxation, business and investments.

Subhash Thakrar, B Comm (Acc) ACA, qualified as a chartered accountant with Spicer & Pegler. He became a partner with Blackstone Franks in 1984.

Other books by Blackstone Franks

Title	Publisher
The UK as a Tax Haven	The Economist Publications Ltd
UK Tax Savings for the Higher Paid	The Economist Publications Ltd
The Economist Guide to the Business Expansion Scheme	The Economist Publications Ltd
Tolley's Business Start Up Packs	Tolley's
The Economist Guide to Management Buy Outs	The Economist Publications Ltd
Crawfords Corporate Finance	The Economist Publications Ltd
Corporation Tax	Oyez Longman
Rasing Finance for Business	The Economist Publications Ltd
Property Taxes	Tolley's
Anti-Avoidance Provisions	Tolley's
Tax Planning for Entertainers	Longman
Tax Minimization Techniques	Oyez Longman
Fringe Benefits	Oyez Longman

INTRODUCTION

The past few years have seen a dramatic change in the financial profile of this country. Increasing numbers of employees with shareholdings in their companies, of retired people, of business-people who have made money and now have capital to invest, are looking for investment opportunities and the best advice on how to use them. Recent legislation in the City and in the financial services industry has made the choice of opportunity very wide; enormous changes have taken place in the investment world, and an environment which was already complex has become even more so. It must not be forgotten, however, that this increased complexity has brought opportunities for the personal investor to improve his or her financial circumstances as never before, and the need for comprehensive information which will help the personal investor make the right decisions has never been greater.

The British education system does nothing to prepare the majority of us for this most important task – that is, to ensure that our capital and savings are safeguarded and protected from the ravages of inflation, the taxman, and ill-considered investment. Many people are at a loss when confronted by the complicated ramifications of the investment world; what they need is information, so that not only can investment opportunities be properly assessed, but professional advisers can be chosen with some confidence.

This book is designed to help; it explains the different investments which exist, their tax implications, and our view of the risk. We have designed a rating system to help the reader evaluate the possibilities, and in our comments have followed the principles which have always guided us in the investment and management of our clients' funds. We avoid the more apparently spectacular options, preferring to concentrate our clients' assets in secure, tax efficient investments which offer a substantially better return than a building society or bank deposit.

Matching a mix of investment options to a particular person's income needs, family responsibilities, capital preservation requirements and tax profile is not a simple matter, and over the years we have developed a level of sound investment practice which we feel is reflected in the advice and judgment given in this book.

We have sought to give information on a variety of matters which the prudent and far-sighted investor would want to consider. What is the best way of protecting dependants if the breadwinner dies early? Are you financially protected in the case of an emergency, such as a serious illness? What kind of health insurance do you need? What is an investment bond? Is it better than a unit trust? How do you make sensible provision for your retirement? What is the best investment for you?

Often, chartered accountants and investment managers seem to be mysterious and secretive about how they arrive at the advice they give; *The Blackstone Franks Good Investment Guide* clarifies all the possible investment opportunities which are available to the personal investor. The entries are indexed alphabetically, and also by rating, so best to worst can be seen at a glance. (See pages 4 to 6.)

This book has not only been written for the personal investor, but should also prove invaluable for the personal financial adviser, as it sets out in a thorough and clear way all the options available for his clients.

This book includes the provisions of the Budget of 17 March 1987.

Blackstone Franks Chartered Accountants
and Investment Managers, 388–396
Oxford Street, London W1N 9HE (01-491 4924)

THE BLACKSTONE FRANKS RATING SYSTEM

£££	Highly recommended
££	Recommended in the right circumstances-not risky
£	Sometimes useful, but risky or limited
?	Depends on your own efforts
XXX	To be avoided - very risky

The rating is only a rough guide, as no simple rating system such as this can be perfect. Markets can 'turn', and our own views would alter depending on world market circumstances.

INDEX BY RATING

£££ Highly recommended

Gilts
Home – your own
Investment bonds
Life assurance
National savings
National savings certificates
National savings deposit bonds
Pensions – company schemes
Pensions – self-administered schemes
Pensions – self-employed
Permanent health insurance (PHI)
Personal equity plans (PEP)
Private medical plans
Retirement annuities
Share option schemes (approved)
Single premium bonds
Term life assurance
Trusts
Trusts – accumulation & maintenance trusts
Umbrella funds
Unit trusts
War loan
Whole life assurance
Wills

££ Recommended in the right circumstances – not risky

Annuities
Annuities to secure endowment policies
'Back to back' arrangements (*see* annuities to secure endowment policies)
Building societies
Capital conversion schemes
Capital gift plan
Deeds of covenant
Endowment policies
Equity linked savings plans
Gilt conversion plans
Guaranteed income bonds
Home income plan
Income & growth bonds
Index linked investments
Investment trusts
Managed or mixed funds

Money market
Maximum investment plans
National savings investment accounts
Offshore funds
Personal accident and sickness insurance
Private medical plans
Quoted securities
School fees planning
Shares
Stock Exchange
Unit linked life assurance
Unit linked savings plans

£ Sometimes useful, but risky or limited

Bank deposits
Business expansion schemes
Certificates of tax deposit
Extra interest accounts
Friendly societies
Gold
Granny bonds
Hospital insurance
Krugerrands
Local authority loans
Local authority stocks or bonds
Premium bonds
Prime residential property funds
Property investment
Unlisted securities market
Woodlands
Zero coupon bonds

? Depends on your own efforts

Antiques
Farms
Holiday lettings
Lloyd's underwriters
Options
Over the counter market
Racehorses
Second homes
Stamps
Wine

XXX To be avoided – very risky

'Angel' investments
Busted bonds
Commodities
Diamonds
Leasing equipment
Limited editions

A

'ANGEL' INVESTMENTS XXX

Investors in stage productions are known as 'angels', and collectively they divide their profits with the management on a percentage basis. For straight plays, the angels may be entitled to 60% of the receipts, and for musicals, 50% after the weekly or monthly 'get out'. The 'get out' is the rent, salaries, publicity, etc, for the period. Usually the first payments are regarded as being the repayment of the capital, with later payments being income.

The income is treated as unearned income, which unfortunately means that if the investor loses money as an angel – and most do – it is difficult to get the loss allowed against other incomes.

Maybe one show in five succeeds, and the recent trend has been for musicals to do well, such as *Cats*. An investment in *Cats* would now be showing a profit in excess of 1,400%. Here are the results of some past shows taken at random:

Show	Gain	(Loss) as %age of capital
Molly		(74%)
Chicago		(100%)
Bodies	66%	
Beatlemania		(100%)
Before the Party		(58%)
Duet for One	45%	
Cats	1,443%	
St Mark's Gospel		(47%)
The Understanding		(100%)
Dial M for Murder		(100%)

If you invested in all of the above shows you would have a profit but only because *one* of the investments was hugely successful – *Cats*. The above figures are as of December 1986.

For more details, write to the Society of West End Theatres, Bedford Chambers, The Piazza, Covent Garden, London WC2E 8HQ. Ask to be put on the 'angels' list.

Blackstone Franks' verdict
This is a risky investment, though some (eg *Cats*, *Evita*) have paid handsomely. You need an angelic attitude when you lose money, as most West End plays fail.

ANNUITIES ££

You hand over a lump sum of money to an insurance company and receive a fixed and regular income guaranteed for life (or a set term). They are often bought by retired people who are prepared to exchange a capital sum for a guaranteed income.

The income you receive is fixed at the time you buy the annuity and is partly determined by the interest rates prevailing at that time. This means annuities are good if you buy when interest rates are high - but not so good to buy when interest rates are low.

The older you are, the higher the income you will receive. However the older you are, the sooner you will die, and so the insurance company are prepared to pay more since they calculate they will make fewer payments. As women live longer than men on average, they receive lower payments than men of the same age.

A great part of the income is tax free as part of the payments is treated as a return of capital. The older you are, the greater the proportion which is tax free. For annuitants in their 90s, for example, all of the income could be tax free.

There are many different types, but you will receive less income if you choose anything other than the standard annuity. For example, you'll get less income if you opt for monthly payments rather than quarterly.

The choices
There are five main choices. The incomes shown below are for an 80-year-old man investing £25,000. The incomes are net of basic rate income tax. The quotes are from three different companies to show just how much variation existed when they were obtained. Altogether, there are about 100 companies which quote annuity rates. Some insurance companies are always near the top of the league for annuities, but the league changes daily as the companies adjust their rates. It is always worth seeking professional advice from an independent adviser who has access to the regular annuity rate surveys made by various organisations.

Quotes for man aged 80, £25,000 invested
Standard
You invest a lump sum to produce an income for the rest of your life. Nothing is paid to your estate if you die, even if you die the day after you bought the annuity.

	Company		
	1	2	3
Monthly income net of basic rate tax	£466	£416	£400

Guaranteed
The income is guaranteed to continue for, say, five years even if you die. The longer the guarantee period, the less income you will receive.

	Company		
	1	2	3
Monthly income net of basic rate tax	£402	£360	£350

Return of excess
If the total income paid out, when you die, is less than the amount invested then the difference is paid to your heirs. Also called capital protected annuity.

	Company		
	1	2	3
Monthly income net of basic rate tax	£380	£362	£345

Increasing annuity
Instead of a fixed income, the income can rise either in line with inflation or by a fixed increase of 3% or 5% per year. The quote is for an increase of 5% per year.

	Company		
	1	2	3
Monthly income net of basic rate tax	£342	£342	£327

Joint life, last survivor
An annuity which is paid to a married couple while both are alive and then continues being paid to the survivor when one partner dies. The income can continue at the same or at a lower level. Quote assumes that each person is aged 80.

	Company		
	1	2	3
Monthly income net of basic rate tax	£389	£293	£284

If the annuity is surrendered, a cash amount can be paid to the individual. In other words, the future income has been exchanged for a capital sum paid today. Alternatively, the income can be assigned to a third party for money, or for an amount paid on the death of the individual entitled to the income. A loan could be made secured against the future income. Each of these events gives rise to a tax liability based on the differences between the amount received and the amount paid for the annuity (as reduced by any capital proportion of annuity payments already received).

Annuities form the basis of other investment devices such as:

Capital conversion schemes
Home income plans
Guaranteed income bonds
School fees planning
Annuity to secure endowment policies (known as 'back to back' arrangements)

(*See* individual sections in this book on the above.)

A purchase of an annuity can save inheritance tax, as the purchase price reduces your estate.

A temporary annuity is one which pays an income for an agreed number of years, eg nine years. This type of annuity is often used in conjunction with annuities to secure endowments, capital conversion schemes, guaranteed income bonds, home income plans, income and growth bonds, and school fees planning.

Blackstone Franks' verdict

Annuities can be a useful way of structuring a source of income for elderly individuals. As a funding arrangement for other related investments, annuities can be most effective. It is worth shopping around as rates vary substantially. They are always better value when interest rates are high.

ANNUITIES TO SECURE ENDOWMENT POLICIES ££
('Back to back' arrangements)

Read the section on annuities, guaranteed income bonds and endowment policies for background.

This can be an alternative to guaranteed growth bonds. An annuity is purchased with a lump sum, and the annuities are used to pay all or part of the endowment assurance premiums on a qualifying policy. Unlike the guaranteed growth bonds, the proceeds of the endowment policy would not give rise to a tax charge after ten years.

Blackstone Franks' verdict

Can be useful in converting taxable income into either tax-free cash or tax-free income after the qualifying endowment assurance matures.

However, capital is locked in, the investment return not always competitive. The annuity ceases on early death but the sum assured under the endowment policy would be payable to your estate and is often calculated to ensure your capital is returned in full in the event of your death.

ANTIQUES

If you purchase wisely, you can enjoy your investments but they bring no regular income and require a substantial investment of your time to visit auctions, shops, etc. Any sale of an antique for less than £3,000 per item is tax free, as long as you invest, rather than trade. A sale of a set of antiques (eg six matching chairs) separately will be treated by the taxman as a single sale of six chairs.

Blackstone Franks' verdict
If you have the time, and know what you're doing, and do not 'trade', then this can be an enjoyable investment. But insure them for replacement value, and expect questions from the taxman if you sell at an auction ... he may want to know if you originally bought the antiques with undisclosed cash income or inherited them without paying inheritance tax. Antiques look nicer than unit trust certificates, but buy for enjoyment, not investment.

B

BANK DEPOSITS £

Interest is paid on your money, and the value of the capital does not fall. If invested within the UK, tax is deducted at source. The interest rate has traditionally not kept pace with inflation, and it is impossible for your capital to grow.

Deposit accounts

Usually seven days' notice is required before a withdrawal can be made. Interest is usually added to the account half-yearly. There are no minimum or maximum deposit limits. If funds are withdrawn before the seven-day notice period, interest may be lost although some banks allow instant withdrawal without loss of interest.

Banks pay a composite rate of tax (currently 25.25%) to the Inland Revenue on interest paid to UK residents. The taxman gives you credit as if basic rate tax (currently 27%) has been paid. If you are a basic rate taxpayer, no further tax is due. If you are liable to higher rates of tax (ie over £16,200 of taxable income), then more tax will be due. Non-taxpayers cannot reclaim the tax withheld, and therefore would be better off to place the deposit offshore (eg Jersey) where no tax is deducted at source, or to invest in a national savings investment.

Some accounts pay interest on a monthly basis, but they require a minimum balance (often about £2,000).

For non-residents of the UK, interest can be paid gross of tax, but note that the Inland Revenue usually require firm evidence that the non-resident pays tax on the deposit account in another country before agreeing that he is non-taxable. In addition, if the non-resident is also not domiciled in the UK, he would be putting his capital at risk unnecessarily to a charge to inheritance tax.

Money market deposit accounts

These accounts pay higher rates of interest, but you must invest a minimum of £10,000. There are two types:

1. *Fixed accounts:* the money is invested for a fixed period, ranging from overnight to five years. You cannot touch your money until the agreed period ends without losing interest. The interest rates are usually higher for longer-term deposits.

2. *Notice accounts:* the deposit is subject to a minimum withdrawal notice period ranging from seven days to six months. Similarly, the bank must give you the same notice if they propose to alter the interest rate.

The interest on both fixed and notice money market accounts is calculated on a daily basis. The rate reflects current money market rates though these rates vary according to the notice period. Like traditional bank deposit accounts, the interest is paid net of basic rate tax (the main exception being investments of £50,000 or more for a period of 28 days minimum, where the interest is paid without any deduction of tax at source).

High interest cheque accounts
These accounts provide you with money market interest rates, but with immediate access to your money with no loss of interest. They also usually provide a cheque book, cheque card and an overdraft facility. A high minimum balance is usually required (between £500 and £2,500, depending on the bank) and if the balance falls below the minimum, either no interest or a reduced rate is payable.

Many accounts set a minimum transaction size of about £250. Some only allow a set number of cheques to be drawn before a charge is made. Interest is paid net of basic rate tax. If you use one of these accounts, it is usually better to write most of your small cheques from your current account, using the high interest cheque account to top up the current account.

Blackstone Franks' verdict
Only good for short-term investments. Not a serious contender for investing lump sums or for saving. Suitable as a temporary home for your money until committed to a longer-term investment.

BUILDING SOCIETIES ££

Building societies offer a range of different investments, but they are mostly competitive with bank deposit accounts paying interest. Although you are unlikely to lose your capital, the return - even after taking into account the lower composite rate of tax payable and the fact that building societies are non-profit making - is less than that made in unit trusts, for instance, in the past few years. Indeed, more funds are now being invested in unit trusts than in building societies.

Like bank deposits, building society accounts can be useful as a home for funds before they are invested permanently.

The tax position is similar to bank deposit accounts. Basic rate tax (currently 27%) is deemed to have been deducted from all interest paid. Thus if you are a basic rate taxpayer only, there will be no further tax to pay. However, if you are a higher rate taxpayer, there will be more tax to pay. This is due on 1 December following the tax year in which the interest is paid. Only the higher rate liability is due, since all building society interest comes with basic rate tax already paid. Non-taxpayers cannot receive a refund of the basic rate tax, so building society accounts are unattractive for such people, including children. Non-resident taxpayers can receive the interest gross, without any tax withheld, but they may have to provide documentary evidence that they declare this interest in their home country. In addition, a non-resident who was also not domiciled in the UK would be putting his capital at risk unnecessarily to inheritance tax.

The net yields on a building society paying 9% net for taxpayers with differing levels of income tax are:

Tax Rate %	After tax yield %
27	9.00
40	7.61
50	6.34
60	5.07

There are four key factors in a building society investment, as in a bank investment, which are:

1. the interest rate offered
2. the minimum investment
3. the notice of withdrawal required
4. the penalties (if any) for early encashment

The lowest interest rates are given on the deposit account and the share account. These accounts are usually only used by solicitors and savings clubs who are forced to invest in absolutely safe accounts.

Blackstone Franks' verdict
Tax-wise, a disaster for the high rate tax payer, even though it is safe. For standard rate taxpayers, with small funds to invest, a safe investment which is easily withdrawn. Generally speaking, one can do better than a building society.

BUSINESS EXPANSION SCHEMES (BES) £

Introduction
Individuals who invest in genuine new equity in qualifying companies can deduct the entire amount of the investment against their taxable income. The maximum allowable investment is

£40,000 per individual per tax year. Husband and wife are treated as one person and the relief is allowable only to outside investors – not for people putting money into their own business or those of their employers. Nor can you invest in companies in which you are a paid director. There is no capital gains tax payable on the eventual sale of the shares. A fuller explanation of the rules can be found in *The Economist Guide to the Business Expansion Scheme* by Blackstone Franks and Co, published by The Economist Publications Limited.

The relief is given against the individual's highest rate of tax. The minimum investment is £500 in any one company and the maximum is £40,000 per annum.

The investor must invest in newly issued shares, not in shares purchased from an existing shareholder. The shares have to be ordinary shares, not preferential shares carrying preferential rights to a dividend or preferential rights to a return of capital.

The investor has to be a resident of the UK, and cannot be an employee of the company.

If you sell the shares within five years, you will lose part or all of the reliefs. The shares are not usually very marketable.

The 1987 Budget allows up to £5,000 to be invested between 6 April and 5 October and to be carried back against taxable income of the previous tax year.

Example

Mr Fowler's total income from all sources is £100,000. His tax position – with and without BES relief of £40,000 – is as follows:

	Without BES relief £		With BES relief £
Income	100,000		100,000
Less: Married allowance	(3,795)		(3,795)
BES relief	-		(40,000)
Total	96,205		56,205
Tax thereon:			
On first £41,200	16,378		16,378
On balance at 60%	33,003		9,003
Total tax	49,381		25,381
Difference (tax saved)		£24,000	

The tax saving may therefore represent 60% of the amount invested.

On the disposal of the shares later than five years after issue, there is no capital gains tax, nor any clawback of the relief.

Conditions

There are over 50 conditions to be met to qualify for relief, and specialist advice should be sought. The main conditions are that the individual investing cannot work for the company or be a husband, wife, parent, or child of the owner of the company, nor be a business partner. Brothers, sisters, uncles and aunts can invest in their relatives' company. Relief is given in the tax year that the shares are issued and fully paid. The company must be unquoted (though OTC and NASDAQ quoted companies are eligible). The company cannot be involved in commodities, selling only to wholesalers, finance businesses generally, a royalty company, farming, property development or an investment company.

Fund or direct?

An investor can either spread the risk by investing in a BES fund, such as those managed by Lazards or Hoare Octagon, or can invest directly in a company. Some funds have failed spectacularly though Lazards and Hoare Octagon have so far been successful.

A direct investment can be made just by investing in a company which is known to you. Alternatively, you can choose an investment from one advertised in the national papers or privately circularised by a stockbroker or a FIMBRA member. Many companies raising BES are newly formed and will not have started trading, and as a result it is very difficult to assess prospects. You should make sure that the directors give you protective undertakings such as limiting their remuneration to agreed levels, not changing the business or its structure, which will lose you the BES relief, future transferability of the shares, etc.

Blackstone Franks' verdict

BES investments are risky, but have tax advantages. For a high rate (60%) taxpayer, merely doubling the value of the shares provides an almost threefold tax-free return on the net after tax investment. Stick to the successful fund managers or a company you really have faith in.

BUSTED BONDS XXX

Collecting busted bonds is also known as scripophily. You collect old share certificates which have been repudiated by the obligor. Some of the common bonds on sale are Russian and Chinese. Recently, some of the Russian bonds suddenly became valuable when the Russians agreed to meet obligations going back to the beginning of the twentieth century. In January 1981, the Chinese Government also agreed to pay on bonds on which they defaulted in 1949. Prices for busted bonds have been volatile, but there are plenty around at low prices (£25 or so).

Blackstone Franks' verdict

They can look attractive when framed and put on the wall. This may be the only pleasure you get from them.

Not a good investment – far too risky.

C

CAPITAL CONVERSION SCHEMES ££

A capital conversion scheme is a method of investing a capital sum to produce 'income' in order to fund premiums to pay on a qualifying life policy. There are several methods available:

1. Temporary annuities. This is described in the section on annuities to secure endowment policies, or back-to-back arrangements.
2. A series of guaranteed income bonds. The returns are guaranteed and this method is convenient.
3. Investment bonds. The return can be quite competitive, as underlying investments are not restricted to fixed interest investment. The main disadvantage is the risk that the value of the investment bond fails to show sufficient growth to pay the premiums. Income limited to 5% of the original investment may be withdrawn without any immediate liability to income tax.
4. A series of low coupon government securities or local authority stocks. The returns here are guaranteed and usually competitive, but the method can be complex.

Blackstone Franks' verdict
An excellent way of converting capital into a larger tax-free sum.

CAPITAL GIFT PLAN ££

This is a new scheme introduced in 1986 to take advantage of the inheritance tax legislation. The capital gift plan aims to provide a way of building up tax-free capital for your beneficiaries while retaining the proposed 'gift' for your own use if necessary. Under the plan, the sum you wish to give is divided into large and small parts. For example, £50,000 would be split into £47,000 and £3,000. The smaller sum is placed in an investment portfolio and written in absolute trust for your nominated beneficiaries – in other words, you have given this sum away forever. However, you can be one of the trustees and can therefore decide when the nominated beneficiaries will receive this sum.

The balance of £47,000 is then passed to the same trustees as an interest-free loan repayable on demand, in part or in whole as required. Thus the trust now has a total of £50,000 to invest, and it would be invested usually in a single premium unit linked investment bond (see separate sections).

The growth and value of the bond provides an increasing capital sum for the beneficiaries as it builds up over the years and is not liable to inheritance tax, regardless of when you die.

The original loan of £47,000 can be withdrawn at any time and remains part of your estate, subject to any tax liability should you die. So, you are in effect simply giving the investment earnings on that sum to your beneficiaries (and not paying tax on those investment earnings as well!).

You could of course pay the entire sum as an outright gift to your beneficiaries, and as long as you survive for more than seven years there will be no inheritance tax. However, only the very wealthy can afford to make such sizeable lifetime gifts outright, and most people might be happier to retain control of the money just in case it is needed for a rainy day.

Blackstone Franks' verdict
Has a definite role to play in inheritance tax planning. At the time of writing, the only capital gift plan in the market was launched by Abbey Life, but we are sure there will be more to follow.

CERTIFICATES OF TAX DEPOSIT £

Certificates of tax deposit is a scheme operated by the Inland Revenue whereby future tax liabilities can be provided for in advance. The deposits are thus guaranteed by the government. The rates vary depending on the amount of the deposit, and whether or not it is eventually used to meet tax liabilities. If you do not use the deposit to pay a tax liability, the interest earned is usually reduced. The interest is paid gross and subject to income tax. Deposits of more than £100,000 should be remitted direct to the Bank of England (drawing office) in London for credit to the general account of the Commissioners of Inland Revenue number 23411007, stating that the money is intended for a certificate of tax deposit, and a copy letter should be sent immediately to the Inland Revenue, Barrington Road, Worthing, West Sussex BN12 4XH. Deposits of less than £100,000 may be made direct to any Collector of Taxes. Details of current rates may be obtained from any tax office.

Blackstone Franks' verdict
The interest rates vary, but usually in a period of falling rates the Inland Revenue's rates are not adjusted quickly and therefore this could be a good investment but only if used to pay tax liabilities. A short dated British Government stock is an alternative, but might not yield as good a return.

COMMODITIES XXX

An investment in commodities could include metals (copper, lead, silver, tin, zinc) or coffee, cocoa, rubber, sugar, oil, soya beans or even pork bellies. A purchase of commodities can be one of two kinds:

1. *Spot goods* are delivered immediately, in which case you have to warehouse and insure the goods.
2. *Future delivery* on an agreed date in the future (a 'future' contract) - you buy (or sell) *now* at a fixed price for delivery at a specified date in the future. If you have bought, and the price increases before you take delivery, you can sell immediately and make your profit. If the price has fallen, however, you can lose your shirt. Every day the price falls, you have to pay your loss into the exchange (called 'margin money') and there is no limit to the potential price collapse, nor is there a limit to how much more money you will have to pay.

Most investment purchases are of futures. A purchase of a future is a purchase of a commodity in, say, six months' time at a predetermined price. The speculator is counting on the price being higher within six months than the agreed price, at which point the commodity is sold prior to its delivery.

Commodities are sometimes classed as 'soft' (eg coffee, sugar) or 'metals' (eg copper, tin).

There are offshore funds which invest directly into commodities (unit trusts are not allowed to invest directly, but do so indirectly by investing in shares of companies connected with commodities). In both cases, however, we consider them to fall into the 'high risk' category.

Alternatively, you can invest with a commodity broker who is given discretion on how to invest your money. He makes the investment decision, and deals with your money on your behalf.

Tax position

The tax position is complex, but can be summarised as:

1. *Physicals.* If you make your own decision and take delivery of the commodity, you are probably carrying on a trade. Your profits are taxable under Schedule D Case I - ie, taxable as earned income. Your losses can be offset against all other income, including that of your spouse.

   If you delegate the decision to a broker, the income will be taxed as Schedule D Case IV - the losses are only deductible against a restricted class of other income, and the profits are treated as unearned income.
2. *Futures.* Profits from futures which are not part of a trade are

taxed as capital gains, and the losses are deductible against all other capital gains.

3. *Unit trusts*. For an onshore unit trust, the gain would be assessed as a capital gain. An offshore fund gain will be taxed as income, however, unless the trust has an agreed 'distributor' status with the Inland Revenue.

Blackstone Franks' verdict

Like the pioneers, you need to be tough. You also need a deep pocket, and a strong gambling instinct even to think about investing here; your losses may not be fully tax deductible. Prices can be extremely volatile.

D

DEEDS OF COVENANT ££

A deed of covenant is a legally binding agreement under which one person promises to make a series of payments to another. You can get tax relief on such payments if the following conditions are met:

1. Neither you nor your spouse benefits from the payment.
2. If the payments are to your own child, he or she must be 18 or over, or married.
3. The payments under the deed must be capable of lasting for more than six years (more than three years for covenants to charities).

Deeds of covenant are especially useful to make payments to your child who is over 18 or to other relatives who need financial support.

Student examples

As an example, you could agree to pay your student child £2,000 a year for seven years, or, if earlier, up to the year in which your child is no longer a student. You pay to your child £2,000 less 27%, ie £1,460. The tax deducted of £540 does not have to be handed over to the Inland Revenue - you keep it. Your child receives the £1,460 but has suffered tax of £540. Since the child has no other income, the £2,000 is lower than the single person's allowance and he or she is therefore entitled to have a full refund of the tax of £540 from the tax man. Thus the child receives a total of £2,000 but it has only cost you £1,460. For further information contact any Inland Revenue office and ask for *Covenants - the Student Tax Information Pack*. You must make sure the payments can be evidenced as having been made, eg by cheque (not cash). There cannot be any reciprocity in setting up covenants, ie where one taxpayer covenants another's child and vice versa. Nor can you make a payment back to the original covenantor to repay them for the covenants.

Apart from student children, deeds of covenant are also popular for:

1. Payments by grandparents or others to minors.
2. Payments to a dependent relative.
3. Payments to a separated spouse before a settlement has been

arranged by the solicitors. This is usually preferable to voluntary maintenance during this period.

Repayment example

As an example of how the repayment is claimed, here is what happens when a parent covenants to his or her student child.

When the deed is made out quoting the gross amount to be paid, it is signed by both parties and witnessed – it is advisable to have it drawn up by a solicitor. The parent completes a form R110 certifying that he or she gets no benefit from making the covenant. Both the deed and form R110 are sent to the student's tax office. A form R185 (AP) is filled out by the parent and the student sends in this form, together with a form R40(S) to reclaim the tax refund. Remember that a covenant is earned income to the student which could mean them paying tax on money earned from holiday jobs.

Blackstone Franks' verdict

Deeds of covenant are particularly useful to make payments to your own student children, grandchildren, godchild or any other child who is not your own, as well as charities and to any relative who does not pay much tax, and needs your support.

DIAMONDS XXX

The diamond industry is heavily influenced by one large company in South Africa (De Beers). They can affect prices. Traditionally, diamonds have not been a good investment. They create no income, you need to insure them, and the price has not kept up with inflation.

Blackstone Franks' verdict

Diamonds may be a girl's best friend, but not if she wants to invest.

E

ENDOWMENT POLICIES ££

What is an endowment policy?
An ordinary term life assurance pays your estate a lump sum on death, but pays nothing if you survive the agreed period. An endowment policy not only pays a lump sum on death, but pays you a tax-free lump sum at the end of the term. In other words, you are bound to get your money back (either dead or alive!). The lump sum can be guaranteed, so you know exactly how much you, or your estate, will receive. An endowment is a way of saving, but you must save for at least 7½ years (and possibly longer) to avoid extra tax charges.

How do you pay?
You pay a premium, usually monthly, throughout the term of the contract. It is not a way of investing a lump sum.

Life assurance element
Endowment policies are not cheap if all you want is life assurance; term or whole life assurance offers better value. However, if you want to save money in a tax effective way, endowment policies offer various advantages.

Advantages of endowment policies

1. Proceeds from a 10 year qualifying policy may be paid to you tax free.
2. Proceeds from qualifying policies which last longer than 10 years can be paid to you tax free after three-quarters of the term or 10 years, whichever is earlier.
3. Policies effected before 14 March 1984 (and which have remained unchanged) attract tax relief on the premiums. If the pre-14.3.1984 policy is varied to increase the benefits or extend the term of insurance, the tax relief will be lost. Variation includes exercising an option to convert to a different kind of policy. The gross premiums of pre-14.3.1984 policies are deductible for income tax purposes up to the higher of £1,500 per tax year or 1/6 of the policy holder's total taxable income.
4. Endowment policies are an excellent way of buying a house! The

proceeds of the policy are applied to repay the house loan, with any surplus proceeds being paid tax free to the householder.

Disadvantages of endowment policies

1. If surrendered before 7½ years you may have a higher rate income tax charge on the proceeds.
2. Surrender values are usually low in the first few years.
3. The income arising on the life company's funds is still liable to corporation tax and capital gains tax.
4. Like all life assurance, you will probably need a medical before you can take out the policy. It is thus unsuitable for the sick or elderly.

Different types of policy

There are several different types, or combinations:

(a) with-profits
(b) without-profits
(c) low cost
(d) pure endowment
(e) unit-linked

(a) With-profits

These policies offer capital appreciation along with the guaranteed sum. The guaranteed sum is increased by regular additions of 'profits' or 'bonuses' declared by the life companies. There are actually two kinds of bonuses:

1. *Regular* (sometimes called 'reversionary') *bonuses*: these are simply added to the guaranteed sum. Thus a bonus of 4% on an original guaranteed sum of £10,000 means that £400 would be added. If the bonus is computed on a compound basis, it is calculated as 4% on the original guaranteed sum *plus* 4% on all bonuses previously given.
2. *Terminal bonuses*: this is a one-off bonus granted on the maturity of the policy (or paid out if the policy becomes a death claim).

The bonuses paid out depend entirely on the results of the life fund, and each company can produce different results. It is very important to select the best life assurance fund, but in reality no-one knows who will perform best in the future. As for past results, here is a table (data extracted from the *Financial Times*, 31 January 1987):

Comparison of maturity values on with-profit endowment contracts

(Man aged 29 at outset, paying gross monthly premium of £30)

(1) 10-year term

Company	Policy started: Dec 1977 Policy matured: Jan 1987 £	Nov 1976 Dec 1986 £	Change %
Clerical Medical	8,943	8,087	+10.6
Friends' Provident	8,577	8,557	+ 0.2
Norwich Union	8,431	7,922	+ 6.4
Scottish Life	7,819	7,549	+ 3.6
Commercial Union	7,529	6,840	+10.1
Sun Alliance	7,368	7,475	- 1.4
Scottish Provident	7,250	6,523	+11.1
GRE	7,121	7,468	- 4.6
Equity & Law	7,093	7,467	- 5.0
General Accident Life	6,812	6,461	+ 5.4
Scottish Equitable	6,519	6,429	+ 1.4
LAS	6,309	6,305	-

(2) 15-year term

Company	Policy started: Dec 1971 Policy matured: Jan 1987 £	Nov 1971 Dec 1986 £	%
Clerical Medical	17,508	15,808	+10.8
Friends' Provident	17,392	17,162	+ 1.3
Norwich Union	17,383	15,750	+10.3
Scottish Life	16,704	15,692	+ 6.4
Equity & Law	15,678	15,270	+ 2.7
Commercial Union	15,313	13,700	+11.8
GRE	15,012	15,401	- 2.5
Sun Alliance	14,985	14,960	+ 0.1
Scottish Provident	14,913	13,286	+12.2
General Accident Life	14,035	12,932	+ 8.5
LAS	13,431	13,406	-
Scottish Equitable	12,960	12,741	+ 1.7

(3) 25-year term

Company	Maturing Jan 1987 £	Maturing Dec 1986 £	Change %
Scottish Life	48,837	43,288	+12.8
Clerical Medical	48,225	45,461	+ 6.1
Norwich Union	48,198	43,594	+10.5
Friends' Provident	47,539	46,497	+ 2.2
Scottish Provident	44,771	39,958	+12.0
Commercial Union	44,767	39,575	+13.1
Equity & Law	43,644	41,389	+ 5.4
GRE	42,619	41,068	+ 3.8
Sun Alliance*	42,348	42,106	+ 0.6
General Accident Life	40,900	34,868	+17.3
LAS	40,045	31,008	+29.1
Scottish Equitable	32,774	32,113	+ 2.1

*Composite figure

As the table shows, investors with the right companies have been well rewarded. A comparison of a building society subscription-share investment of £30 per month with the above endowment policy results shows the following:

	Best endowment return £	Worst endowment return £	Building society £
10-year term	8,943	6,309	5,628
15-year term	17,508	12,960	10,683

Remember, past results are no guarantee of future success. Today's failure can be tomorrow's success, and vice versa.

Despite these results, most with-profits endowments are linked almost entirely to the house mortgage market. The guaranteed lump sum is used to repay the building society loan, and the tax-free profits are then kept by the house owner. Very few people are saving via endowment policies unless they are linked to a house purchase.

(b) Without-profits

While the premiums are much lower than in a with-profits policy, the sum assured remains the same throughout the period. As it cannot increase, it will offer no inflation protection. This kind of policy is not generally recommended as the rate of return is poor.

(c) Low cost
This was developed as a way of buying a house, and consists of two policies:

1. *With-profits endowment:* has a sum assured which is *less* than the outstanding capital under the mortgage, but by the maturity date the additional profits will have increased the sum assured sufficient to repay the loan.
2. *Decreasing term assurance:* provides repayments of any shortfall under the endowment policy should death occur before the maturity date. The low cost endowment is a cheaper way of repaying a mortgage.

(d) Pure endowment
These are rarely used as they exclude all death benefit, and only pay a sum at full maturity.

(e) Unit-linked
The unit-linked endowments will pay a guaranteed lump sum if you die during the policy term. Part of the premium goes to buy term insurance, the rest buys units in one or more investment fund. The usual insurance company funds are equity, international, property, gilts, cash and managed funds. The sum assured reflects the underlying value of the particular units held.

Switches between funds can be made, the first in a year usually being cost-free and thereafter subject to a charge of about £15 to £25 per switch. If you don't want to decide which funds to invest in, the managed fund appoints fund managers to decide when and what fund switches should be made, and what proportion of your premiums should be invested in which funds.

Whereas with a with-profits policy there is a guaranteed sum assured, this is not the case with unit-linked. The sum assured on a unit-linked policy is dependent solely on the value of the units, and these can fall as well as rise. In recent years, unit-linked has performed far better than the with-profits policy – the extra risk has resulted in greater rewards.

Life cover is generally cheaper than a with-profits contract as the insurance companies themselves believe that the unit-linked policy will out-perform the with-profits type.

Unit-linked endowment policies can offer an option to take a tax-free income after 10 years. The capital sum can remain in the fund, part surrenders to the policy holder being made as and when required. This can be particularly useful to provide for school fees, or supplement a pension, or increase the net spendable income of a higher rate taxpayer. This option can be attractive to a higher rate taxpayer in particular, since the funds retained by the life assurance company will be paid, tax free, to the individual (though the income would still be taxed at the life assurance company rates).

The alternative would have been for the high rate taxpayer to invest the funds himself and suffer higher rate tax on the resulting income. This, however, should be contrasted with investing in unit trusts which is likely to be better still, as unit trusts are exempt from tax on capital gains, though the investor remains liable when the units are sold.

'Joint lives, first death' – 'Last survivor'

Endowment policies can be written under 'Joint lives, first death' or 'Last survivor'. This distinction is important when a life policy is written jointly on both the husband's and the wife's lives.

'*Joint Lives, First Death*' means the sum assured is paid on the first death of one of the joint lives assured. In other words, if the joint lives are husband and wife, the sum assured is payable on the first death.

'*Last Survivor*' is the opposite – the sum assured is payable on the *second* death of the lives assured. This is a cheaper policy than either a single life, or joint lives, first death policy.

Premiums are lower if you are younger, and premiums based on women's lives usually cheaper than men's (as they live longer). Smokers pay extra.

Early surrender

The effects of pulling out of an endowment policy early can be severe. There are tax charges (see below) and the surrender value is low – indeed, you may not even get all of your money returned. An alternative to surrender is to make it a paid-up policy. This means that no further premiums are payable, but you have to wait until maturity to get paid. The benefits are reduced, of course, as you will have paid fewer premiums.

The taxation consequences of early surrender are:

1. Part or all of the tax relief on premiums is clawed back if surrendered within four years.
2. Potential charge to higher rate tax on surrender of policy (either part or all surrendered).
3. Cashing of bonuses on with-profits policies is treated as part surrender.

Blackstone Franks' verdict

Can be used for building up a lump sum or paying off a mortgage, but is not applicable if you want to invest a lump sum. As with other forms of life insurance, it is important not only to match the type of insurance required to the individual's needs, but also to select the right company. Unit-linked life assurance may be a better alternative. An average 10-year with-profits policy has shown a tax-free return of over 11% per annum, with the top companies producing a return of 20% per annum.

EQUITY LINKED SAVINGS PLANS ££

See unit-linked savings plans.

EXTRA INTEREST ACCOUNTS £

Extra interest accounts is a term used by banks and building societies for accounts which pay extra interest, usually because the money is locked up for a longer time. They are also known as high interest accounts. Read the sections on banks and building societies for a full explanation.

F

FARMS ?

It is often thought that owning a farm is a good investment, but this is highly questionable. The income from a farm, in relation to its capital value, is very low. The income is also dependent on the weather, and the ability of the farm managers, and can be affected by disease. Farmers in Europe and the USA are having a tough time financially, and some are being declared bankrupt.

Blackstone Franks' verdict
Only for the hardy.

FRIENDLY SOCIETIES £

Friendly societies give small investors a means of investing in a tax-free fund similar to that of a pension fund. A registered friendly society has a variety of tax advantages.

However, the amount that can be invested is so small that it is not usually worth bothering with.

Friendly societies have one major advantage over life companies – they can offer tax exempt policies where the investments are not only free of capital gains tax, but also income tax, and the entire proceeds of the policy can be paid to the investor tax free. These policies have to be for 10 years, and require regular premiums. Unfortunately, the amount of life cover is restricted to a mere £100 of annual premiums (about £8.30 a month).

Some societies allow you to invest a lump sum (of about £1,000) which enables you to pay the premiums in advance, and this is then fed into the plan over the following 10 years.

At least half of the funds have to be invested in 'narrow range securities' which means fixed interest investments, eg gilts, building society deposits, bank deposits, etc. The remaining half may be invested in 'wider range securities', ie equities.

Friendly society schemes have other limitations – an investor can only have one plan, and if surrendered before the end of 10 years only the premiums paid can be refunded, no other profit.

The societies have been described as an anachronism in the present age. They flourished in the Victorian era under the principles of thrift and mutual self-help. Nonetheless, the tax protection given to the policies is only perhaps equalled by a personal equity plan (PEP).

Blackstone Franks' verdict
The most you can invest is £100 per annum, which makes this investment not worth bothering with. While the £100 investment is completely free of tax, so is a PEP (personal equity plan) where you can invest £2,400 per annum (£4,800 for a married couple). Forget friendly society investments.

G

GILT CONVERSION PLANS ££

See capital conversion schemes.

GILTS £££

Gilts are publicly quoted stocks backed fully by the British Government. The name gilt comes from the original certificates which were issued with gilded edges. At no time has a British Government failed to meet any of its funded debt obligations whether in the nature of capital or income. But don't be fooled into thinking that gilts are always safe. If you have to sell before maturity, you can lose a lot of money. How much you lose or gain depends on what has happened to interest rates.

When you buy a gilt, you are lending the government money for a guaranteed interest rate (called the 'coupon'). Repayment is set at a specified date, so you can work out exactly how much you will receive, and when.

Rates of return are often higher than from a bank or building society, and the guarantee is stronger – the government is less likely to go bankrupt than Barclays Bank or Abbey National.

Small investors have avoided gilts for several reasons. First, they appear complicated. This is true, but we hope that this section will explain how they work, and in particular the *Blackstone Franks' Gilt Rules* should be useful. Gilts come in different shapes and sizes. They differ in prices, rates of return and maturity dates.

The second reason gilts have been avoided is inflation. In the years 1945–1980 gilts were a poor investment. Indeed, the real rate of return has sometimes been negative, as inflation rates have far exceeded the interest rates earned. This is true of any fixed rate investment, including bank and building society deposits. Third, gilts can lose you money if you sell them before maturity and interest rates have risen (which, as explained below, will reduce the price).

Gilts are a good investment to meet a future known liability, or to obtain a fixed return on capital.

Some background

The amount of trading that occurs in the gilts market each day is enormous – it amounts to around £1,000,000,000 a day. Most of this trading is carried out by large financial institutions such as pension funds and life assurance companies, though individuals also buy them. About 17% of gilt deals by volume are by individuals, with an average deal of £32,000.

Gilts go by different names, but these names have no real meaning from an investment point of view (eg Exchequer or Treasury or War Loan). A gilt edge stock might be termed, for example, 'Treasury 9½% 1999'. This means that the stock will be redeemed (paid back) in 1999 and that the interest rate (the coupon) per £100 nominal stock is 9½%.

Prices of gilts are always quoted per £100 nominal, since the government will always repay £100 when the redemption date arrives. This £100 is sometimes called 'par value' or 'face value' or 'nominal value'.

Why prices of gilts vary with interest rates

All gilts have a redemption price of £100, yet if you look at their prices in the 'British Funds' or 'Gilts' section of a newspaper, none would cost £100. Because gilts are just traded as assets, they are in competition with other interest bearing assets, such as bank deposits and building society accounts. Their price has to vary with market rates of interest to make it attractive for people to hold them.

First example

A gilt has an 8% coupon.
The market rate of interest is 10%.
What is the price of the gilt?

Answer:

The price of the gilt must be such that it yields 10%, not 8%.

That price is £80, since the coupon (£8) will yield a return of 10% only if the price of the gilt is £80. This is because an £8 return on an investment of £80 gives a 10% yield.

Second example

What happens to the price of the gilt if interest rates
(a) increase to 12%?
(b) decrease to 8%?

Answer (a):

An £8 return has to yield 12%. The price of the gilt will therefore *fall* to £66.66, since £8 on £66.66 invested yields a 12% return.

Answer (b):

An £8 return has to yield 8%. The price of the gilt will therefore *rise* to £100. An £8 return on an investment of £100 is a yield of 8%.

Thus, if interest rates *rise*, the price of gilts *falls*, whilst if interest rates *fall*, the price of gilts *rises*.

The true yield

If the price of Treasury 9½% 1999 is £92, then the real interest rate is more than the 9½% coupon. A return of £9.50 on an investment of £92 is more like 10.33%, not 9½%. This is because the coupon is based on the £100 nominal figure, not the price which you actually pay. The real return of 10.33% is known as the yield. If you then take into account that in 1999 you will obtain not £92 but £100 (an additional £8), as well as all the interest during those years, then the yield is really somewhat higher - in this example, it is 10.89% yield including the extra £8. This yield is know as the gross redemption yield.

Low and high, short, medium and longs

Gilts can be categorised by the value of the coupon - 3% 1990-95 is a 'low coupon' stock, whereas Treasury 15¼% 1996 is 'high coupon'. Gilts which have less than five years to run before maturity are 'shorts', whereas those which are redeemable between five and 15 years from now are 'medium', and if over 15 years to maturity they are known as 'longs'.

Redemption dates

A redemption date 1990/95 means that the government can redeem this stock at any time between those two dates, though normally the latest possible date is chosen. There are even undated stocks - for example, Consoles 2½% has never been redeemed, and was first issued in 1752.

Index-linked

Some gilts are index-linked. The indexing is reflected in a higher redemption value, but the interest rate is much lower.

Interest, gains and tax

Interest payments on gilts are made twice a year, and are taxable income for UK residents. The profit made from the rise in price of gilts is tax free as a capital gain. The higher the rate of tax you pay, the better it is to have a low coupon gilt since the bulk of the profits will not come from taxable interest, but from tax-free capital gain. Note that if you lose money on your gilt investments, the loss is not deductible either as a capital loss or as an income loss.

Non-residents

On a number of gilts, there is no tax due either on income or capital gain if you are not resident in the UK, though you may have to prove to the Inland Revenue that you declare the gilts to to the tax people in your foreign country. It is not enough simply to provide a foreign address. The Inland Revenue require proof that you are a taxpayer elsewhere before they authorise the Bank of England to pay you gross. In order to obtain approval, you should obtain Form A3 from the Inspector of Foreign Dividends, Lynwood Road, Thames Ditton, Surrey, KT7 0DP. Unless you have already been cleared as non-resident, expect some searching questions about your long-term plans, duration of visits, location of home, and so on.

Blackstone Franks' gilt rules

Rule 1 If you think interest rates are about to rise, then either do not buy gilts or apply rule 2 carefully.

Rule 2 If you want to avoid gambling on interest rates, only buy gilts which you will hold until maturity, otherwise you can lose a lot of money if you sell the gilts too early in a time of rising interest rates.

Rule 3 If you want to gamble on interest rates falling, buy long-dated or medium-dated gilts.

Rule 4 If you believe strongly that inflation will return, or you want to pay for the extra protection of inflation-proofing, buy only index-linked gilts.

Rule 5 If you are a low rate taxpayer, buy high coupon gilts. If you are a high rate taxpayer, buy low coupon gilts.

Unit trusts

There are more than 60 gilt and fixed interest unit trusts, with over £500 million invested in this way. Unit trusts are explained in more detail later in this book. The unit trusts are rather inactive, since if the managers trade too frequently they can run foul of the Inland Revenue who will withdraw their tax advantages if the trust attempts to convert income into capital gain (a process known as bond washing). In addition, the trust charges are considered high with a usual initial charge of 5%, which is far more than the charge of dealing direct. Some unit trusts have eliminated the initial charge, replacing it with a more modest annual management fee of, say, 0.75% with a minimum investment of £1,000. Fidelity, Abbey and Mercury are all trusts which reduce their charges, though Fidelity also offer a monthly income facility. Fidelity have also abolished the spread between the buying and selling price, and claim that they are a cheaper way of buying gilts than the Post Office.

Blackstone Franks' verdict

Although gilts are backed by the British Government, the prices can be volatile. Can be useful as part of a portfolio, especially where it is felt that interest rates will fall. Useful for investing a lump sum which has to be used to meet a known future obligation. Index-linked gilts and low coupon gilts favour higher rate tax payers.

GOLD £

Gold is thought to be a wonderful asset in times of political upheaval. However, prices have been very volatile. The Americans and the Russians have huge hoards of gold, worth many times the amount of gold traded in any year worldwide. Thus if they sold from their stockpiles, they could easily depress the price of gold.

You can purchase gold by buying gold coins (*see* Krugerrands) or gold bars. You could also purchase gold shares or unit trusts which specialise in gold shares.

Alternatively, Citibank have an international 'certificate program' under which you can decide how much you want to spend on gold or silver in your local currency (with a minimum equivalent of $1,000). The bank collects all the orders received daily and makes purchases at the going market rate, which is then divided up amongst the contributors. You receive a certificate stating how much you have been allocated. You can either take delivery or leave it in storage at the point of purchase. There are no storage fees for the first year; thereafter 0.75% of the value is charged. A commission of 3% is payable and a further 1% if you decide to take delivery or sell.

The advantage of this scheme is that the spread between buy and sell prices is much narrower than if you deal with a bullion broker. At the same time you can pay by credit card or cheque. Details are available from Citibank in New York on 212-559 6041.

Blackstone Franks' verdict
'As good as gold' should be rephrased: 'as risky as gold' is more accurate.

GRANNY BONDS £

Granny bonds were a form of national savings certificates, called retirement issue, which were only available to people of retirement age, hence the popular name. They are now open to everybody. (*See* national savings certificates.) The certificates were, in effect, index-linked. While inflation was at a high level these certificates produced very good protection of capital, but as inflation has fallen (by 17% pa over 6–7 years) the certificates' worth as investments has diminished.

Blackstone Franks' verdict
Better value may be had from the range of national savings options available.

GUARANTEED INCOME BONDS ££

To understand this section, you should read the section on annuities first.

Guaranteed income bonds consist of the purchase of two separate annuity contracts.

An example best illustrates what happens:

A 65-year-old purchases a 10-year guaranteed income bond for £10,000. This actually comprises a 10-year temporary annuity costing £5,500 and a deferred annuity contract costing £4,500.

The 10-year temporary annuity produces £1,000 per year for 10 years. This represents 10% of the initial outlay. The annuity payments consist of £700 of capital and £300 of income. The £300 of income would be subject to income tax.

When the temporary annuity ends after 10 years, the investor will have the option of either taking a life-time annuity under the second contract of, say, £1,600 per annum, or a lump sum equal to the initial capital outlay, ie £10,000. Thus income is guaranteed throughout the 10-year period, and the investor can have all of his capital returned.

See also section on income and growth bonds.

Blackstone Franks' verdict

A guaranteed income which can suit the elderly in the right circumstances. If you think interest rates will fall over a 10-year period, they may be worth buying.

H

HOLIDAY LETTINGS ?

A commercial furnished holiday letting offers numerous tax advantages if certain conditions are met. The conditions are:

1. The lettings must be commercial with a view to making a profit.
2. The lettings must be furnished.
3. The property must be available to the general public for periods totalling at least 140 days in a tax year and must be let for at least 70 days.
4. The property must not normally be let to the same person for more than 31 days.
5. If the investor owns more than one property, and each property has not been let for 70 days, an averaging may be made.
6. The property must be in the UK: overseas property is excluded.

The advantages are:

1. The income is treated as earned income. This enables you to pay more into a pension fund. (See page 77 for the advantages of pensions for the self-employed.)
2. Retirement relief for capital gains tax purposes can be claimed. This means the first £125,000 of capital gains is tax-free once you are over 60 years old.
3. Roll-over relief from capital gains tax can be claimed. This means a capital gain on the sale of a holiday home can be 'rolled over' into another asset.
4. The income can be divided between husband and wife (by forming a partnership), and an election can be made for separate taxation to avoid the higher rates of income tax.
5. Wife's earned income relief can be utilised.
6. Any losses can be offset against all other income.
7. Capital allowances (ie tax deductions) may be claimed for equipment, fixtures and fittings.
8. Interest borrowing for the purposes of the business would be deductible.
9. The assets attract business property relief, which reduces the liability to inheritance tax.

Blackstone Franks' verdict

Has the advantage of riding the increases in capital values of property, but requires careful selection and good management to succeed. Returns can be low, and investors should be wary of borrowing too much to purchase properties until the income has been proven and is capable of servicing the debt. Good tax advantages, though, and attractive for retired people who wish to be active in managing their investments.

HOME – YOUR OWN £££

If you don't own your own home, you will be paying rent. Buying your own home is, in our opinion, the best investment you can make. Your mortgage, up to £30,000, is tax deductible. The gain you make on your house is entirely tax free. There are a variety of different mortgages on the market. Careful selection of the correct mortgage basis is essential.

Owning your own home can have snags. You must have a full, written survey. You must take out complete insurance. You should use a qualified adviser, such as a solicitor, to complete the purchase. Some areas have proven to be poor investments, such as Aberdeen, where prices fell by 30% in 1986. If you change house (or flat) often, having renovated them, the Inland Revenue may seek to tax your profits as a 'trade', even though it is also your only residence. On balance, however, your own home can prove to be an excellent investment.

This does not mean to say that a house is a good investment for investing a lump sum once you already own your own home.

Blackstone Franks' verdict
Buying your own home is a great investment.

Investing in a second home (or even more) can be a good investment, but the Rent Acts are weighted against landlords. There are easier ways of investing in property – *see* property investment.

HOME INCOME PLANS ££

See also annuities.

Home income plans allow the elderly to unlock the capital in their house. There are three main schemes:

1. Mortgage/annuity plans
2. Reversion annuity
3. Reversion property bonds

Mortgage/annuity plan
The basis of a home income plan is similar to an annuity. It allows an individual to use the substantial value of the house in which they may have lived for some years to generate additional income during

retirement, but at the same time being able to live rent-free in the house.

The householder borrows a proportion of the value of the house from an insurance company. The loan is secured by a mortgage over the property. That loan is then used immediately to purchase an annuity. Part of the annuity is used to pay the interest on the mortgage loan, whilst the other part provides the additional income. The capital of the loan is not repaid until after death. To avoid fluctuations, the loan is a fixed interest mortgage.

If the loan is made to a person who has attained the age of 65, the interest on the loan is eligible for tax relief. The maximum amount of the loan which is eligible for tax relief is £30,000, and is unlikely to exceed 80% of the value of the house. The property must be in the UK and be the only or main residence at the time the interest is paid. The interest must be paid by the person to whom the loan is made. Note that ownership of the house is not lost under this scheme although there is, of course, a new large loan outstanding against the property.

Reversion annuity
Under these plans you sell your house, or a portion of it, at full vacant possession valuation and buy an annuity with the proceeds. You and your spouse are granted guaranteed legal rights to stay in the property until you die, in exchange for a nominal rent of £1 a month.

As there is no loan involved, there is no mortgage interest to pay and the net return will be much higher than the first method described above. However, you lose ownership of the house, and lose your stake in any future increase in the value of that house.

Reversion property bonds
You sell your house to a life insurance company at a sitting tenant valuation in exchange for units in the company's residential property fund. This is clearly a much lower valuation than the usual market valuation which assumes vacant possession. You are granted guaranteed life occupation. You can withdraw up to 5% of the units in the fund tax free each year. On your death, the value of the investment bond is added to your estate. The plan can be activated at any age. The bond participates indirectly in overall future house price increases, since the fund consists of residential property, including your house. However, under this scheme you have sold your house.

Blackstone Franks' verdict
For the elderly, who are short of income, this is one solution, but bear in mind the effect of having 'sold' your home. Consider other alternatives first.

HOSPITAL INSURANCE £

See also permanent health insurance, personal accident and sickness insurance, and private medical insurance.

The purpose of this insurance is to provide you with sufficient funds to offset part of your loss of earnings while in hospital and also to cover incidental expenses such as the cost of relatives' travel to and from hospital. In addition, the plan might usually provide further benefits such as a lump sum for the loss of a limb or eyesight. While no medical evidence is usually required before a plan is effected, there could be problems if a claim is made against a condition which existed when the policy was taken out. Most companies will not pay out benefits during the first two years of the policy if the claim relates to a recurrence of an illness which you have previously had. The taxation treatment of any benefits received is similar to personal accident and sickness insurance, ie the lump sum benefits are usually tax free with the income benefits being tax free until received for one full tax year.

Blackstone Franks' verdict

Does not provide much protection - permanent health insurance is better.

I

INCOME AND GROWTH BONDS ££

Income and growth bonds are investments issued by insurance companies which are suitable for lump sums. You have to invest your money for a fixed period - perhaps 5 or 10 years - but it can be as little as 2 years. In return you get a fixed rate of interest which is paid net of basic rate of tax. They are often called guaranteed bonds.

With an *income bond*, the return is paid out as a regular income (usually twice a year). A *growth bond* accumulates the return, which is paid out when the bond comes to an end.

If you die before the bond comes to an end, the insurance company normally pays out the amount you originally invested plus, with growth bonds, the return accumulated to date.

There are various types of bonds, and they can depend on your tax position. The bonds are primarily a form of annuity investment (*see* separate section on annuities).

Guaranteed income bonds are described in more detail in a separate section. *See also* capital conversion schemes.

Blackstone Franks' verdict

Very good for lump sum investments. There are many different types and combinations on the market and you must select the one which best suits your own requirements and tax position. Independent professional advice is essential to select the right bond. Frequently better than building society returns, and a good buy when you expect interest rates to fall during the period of the bond. Your money is, however, 'locked in'.

INDEX-LINKED INVESTMENTS ££

There are some national savings investments which guarantee that the buying power of the money you invest will keep pace with rising prices. The section on national savings certificates discusses the index-linked ones.

When the index-linked certificates were first issued, they were only available to people aged 50 or over, and replaced the Retirement Issue (popularly known as granny bonds because, when first issued, they were only available to people of retirement age).

Some Gilts are also index-linked (see separate section).

Blackstone Franks' verdict
Can be reasonably safe, especially in times of high inflation.

INVESTMENT BONDS £££

Investment bonds are a form of lump sum investment with an insurance company. They are sometimes called single premium bonds since you pay one premium at the beginning, rather than an annual premium. The usual minimum investment is £500 to £2,000 and one can normally add to it in increments of £250 to £1,000.

An investment bond is technically a non-qualifying single premium life assurance policy. There is only a limited amount of life assurance, normally equivalent to the value of your bond and not less than the original sum invested.

You do not get an income in the conventional sense of having interest paid to you. The income earned by the fund's investments is generally put back into the fund for more investment. Instead, you can arrange to cash in part of your investment from time to time either on a regular basis or as and when you require cash. This income is potentially tax free, and can be paid to you monthly, quarterly, half-yearly, or annually – or even each term if it is being used to pay school fees. In general you will not pay any tax if you withdraw no more than 5% of your original investment each year. To make it easier to get an income, bonds are sold as a cluster or series of identical mini-policies, so that you can cash in a whole policy or several at a time according to your needs. The tax rules with a cluster or series are simpler.

The units
Generally when you invest, your money buys the units in a fund of investments run by the insurance company. The price of each unit you buy is roughly the value of the investments in the fund divided by the total number of units issued. The unit price goes up and down as the value of investments in the fund fluctuates (eg property, shares, etc). The insurance company makes a charge of 5%, usually, against the funds invested.

When you sell your units, you get back the price of the units at that time. If the fund has performed badly, you will make a loss. On the other hand, if the fund does well, you stand to make a large profit. There are two prices for the units: the offer or buying price, and the bid or selling price. The bid price is usually 5% less than the offer; both are quoted in the newspapers. For investments beyond a certain amount (say £10,000), the buyer may be allocated extra units and the insurance company may give up some of its 5% initial charge.

Most insurance companies run a number of funds, and you can usually choose which fund, or which mixed funds, you invest in. The usual funds are:

Property funds – Investing in office blocks, factories, shops and prime residential property.
Equity funds – Investing in shares either directly or via unit trusts or investment trusts.
Fixed interest funds – Investing in things which pay out a fixed income (eg British Government stocks, local authority bonds).
Managed funds – Investing in a mixture of property shares, fixed interest investments, etc.
Cash funds – Investing in bank deposit accounts, short-term loans to local authorities and other investments which are similar.

You can also invest in units which specialise in particular regions, eg Far East, America, Europe.

You can follow the fortunes of your investments by looking up the unit price in the financial press under the section *insurance bonds*.

Whether you invest by a single investment bond, or a unit-linked savings plan, you need to choose the right company, with a sensible policy document. For example, the price can be affected by how the fund is valued, whether an independent valuer was used, the maximum period between valuations, how the unit prices are worked out, the charges the company makes, and what happens to the funds' income.

Investment bonds *vs* unit trusts

Investment bonds and unit trusts both offer professional management and a spread of investments. There are some important differences, however:

1. Investment bonds have unusual tax consequences which are set out below. As a result, they should be seen as a long-term investment. You could face a large income tax liability if you encash the bond in a year of high income.
2. Unit trusts do not pay any capital gains on their profits within the trusts, whereas investment bonds do. On the other hand, the sale of unit trusts is liable for capital gains tax; when an investment bond is encashed, there is no capital gains tax.
3. You can take 5% per annum from the investment bond tax free (the tax is explained in more detail below). However, many unit trusts offer a similar withdrawal scheme.
4. Unlike unit trusts, switching your investments between funds (eg from equity funds to property funds) can be done at a very low cost with no tax being payable as a result. Normally one switch per year is free, with a charge of, say, £10 to £20 for additional switches.

5. As a unit trust is not a life policy, there is no life cover attached to it as there is with an investment bond. On death, the amount received will be the greater of the life cover or the bid value of the units in the bond fund. Sometimes the amount of the life cover depends on the age at death; it might be 2.5 times the bid value of units on death at age 30, dropping to just over the value of the units at age 70. This can be seen as a disadvantage, as part of the investment monies are being used to fund life cover, which is not the case with unit trusts. It also means that there are adverse rates for older investors who are not in the best of health.
6. Investment bonds can be quite useful for individuals whose income fluctuates from year to year. In good income years instead of taking the 5% tax free, it can be deferred. So if the individual has four good income years but then a poor one, in the fifth year 25% of the original investment can be taken tax free.
7. The higher rate tax charge on withdrawing over 5% can be substantially reduced or eliminated by taking that income in a year when you are only liable for tax at the basic rate.
8. An investment bond can be used to avoid inheritance tax. A child or grandchild, for instance, could be the beneficiary instead of the investor. This would avoid inheritance tax on the growth in value of the bond. Inheritance tax may be applied at the time of buying the bond, but professional advice should be taken to clarify this.
9. A bond can be advantageous to a trust as it is a non-income producing asset. There is no tax liability on the trust or the beneficiaries until the bond is finally cashed. The trust instrument must give the trustees power to invest in a non-income producing asset and the power to invest in life assurance policies before an investment bond can be purchased.
10. Investment bonds can be useful for accumulation and maintenance trusts, and as gifts to children since they render 5% tax-free income.
11. It is possible to exchange a portfolio of stocks and shares for units in a bond fund. The same possibility exists with unit trusts. This avoids the normal cost of selling securities, but creates a potential capital gains tax liability. Usually higher prices for the shares can be obtained in an exchange and reinvestment in the bond fund can be made immediately, without waiting for the next Stock Exchange settlement date.
12. Investment bonds can be used for children under the age of 18 with capital provided by their parents. This is an advantage because if the capital was invested in another way the resulting income would be aggregated with that of the parents to determine the tax liability.

13. Because the investment bond is whole life assurance, it will mature on the death of the person whose life is assured. A married couple may have such an investment written on their joint lives to mature on the death of the survivor. This defers the tax payment until the second death and allows the survivor a tax-free income after the death of the first person.
14. Full-time professional management is obtained. The investment bonds are permitted to invest in a wider range of assets than unit trusts. For example, a unit trust cannot invest in cash deposit funds.
15. On death, the unit trust holder's estate does not suffer a charge to higher rates of tax as may be the case with an investment bond; in addition, the unit trust shares will be completely free of capital gains tax.

The tax position

The investor can withdraw 5% of the original investment per annum over a period of 20 years tax free. These withdrawals need not be taken each year, and may be postponed and accumulated as a 'tax-free' allowance to be taken in later years.

Any amount withdrawn in the first 20 years in excess of the cumulative allowance of 5% per annum will give rise to a potential tax liability (as will withdrawals after 20 years) but only to higher rates of tax, not standard rates, and 'top slicing' relief is available.

In calculating the tax when the policy is cashed in, 'top slicing relief' is computed to reduce your tax bills. If you are a basic rate taxpayer, there is no further tax to pay. The gain on the bond is divided by the number of complete years for which the policy has been in force. The resulting amount is then added to your total income arising in the year of encashment. The top rate of tax payable for that year is thus determined. The basic rate is then deducted from this higher rate and this 'excess' rate is then applied to the whole of the gain on the bond. Similar calculations are made when the policy is partially cashed in over the 5% allowance.

If you are going to cash in more than 5% per annum, the tax charge can be avoided, and greater flexibility achieved, by taking out a series of smaller bonds instead of one large bond. In this way you can encash a small bond instead of making a partial encashment of a large bond, with possible penal tax consequences.

Unlike unit trusts, the insurance company pays capital gains tax on the gains made in an investment bond, and this is taken into account in arriving at the unit price.

If you are 65 or older, the cashing in of the bond could affect entitlement to age allowance. If the profit from the bond, together with other income, exceeds £9,400, the age allowance is reduced by £2 for every £3 of the excess - so you pay extra tax. In these circumstances, top slicing is not allowed.

Blackstone Franks' verdict
Investment bonds can be very useful to generate a tax-free income and to link it with a variety of different types of investment. The flexibility of being able to switch from one fund to another is very useful. Bonds should be encashed in the tax year when your income is low due to retirement, employment overseas or unemployment. You should also consider the advantages of a series of small bonds. Investment bonds can be useful for trusts, as described above. If you are likely to want all of your money back at short notice, bonds should be avoided as they are a medium - longer term investment. Over the past 15 years, unit trusts have grown very popular because they have been seen as marketable investments, which is not a commitment for the long term. On the other hand, if you buy an investment bond and take your 5% each year, you can forget about taxation for up to 20 years.

INVESTMENT TRUSTS ££

Investment trusts are not trusts, but companies. They invest in other companies' shares, fixed interest securities, property, or even in cash deposits. Investment trusts spread the risk by investing in many different stocks and shares. When you buy a share in an investment trust, you get a share of the underlying portfolio owned by the investment trust. In this way, they are similar to unit trusts which also invest in other investments. However, there are differences.

Differences between investment trusts and unit trusts

1. The share price of an investment trust moves up and down depending on demand and supply for the shares. The share price does not reflect the value of investments which they own - indeed, they usually sell at a discount to the underlying investment. Unit prices for a unit trust are calculated strictly according to the value of the underlying investment.
2. Unit trusts are 'open ended', but investment trusts are 'closed end' funds. This may seem unimportant, but it is not. Managers of investment trusts know how much money they can invest, whereas managers of unit trusts are subject to the whims of the public in investing, or withdrawing, from their funds. Individuals can, of course, sell their investment trust shares, but they sell them to other buyers, rather than redeeming them from the managers. The consequence of this is that investment trust managers are less concerned if they buy long-term, unmarketable investments as they do not have to stay as liquid as the unit trust manager. The unit trust manager is legally obliged to buy back his units and may have to sell some of the fund's investments to cope with redemptions. Because investment trusts cannot be forced to redeem their shares, they can

take a longer-term view on investments and invest in less liquid investments, eg shares in unquoted companies or property. Unit trusts are forbidden to invest in such assets.

3. An investment trust must distribute at least 85% of the income it receives to its shareholders. On the other hand, it must reinvest its capital gains and cannot distribute them to shareholders.
4. Investment trusts cannot invest more than 15% of their assets in any one security, whereas unit trusts are restricted to 5%.
5. An investment trust can borrow, whereas a unit trust cannot.
6. Unit trusts are restricted to investing in quoted securities, ie companies quoted on the Stock Exchange. Investment trusts are more flexible and can invest in property, treasury bills, bank deposits, etc.
7. Investment trusts are not allowed to advertise except when they first issue their shares. Unit trusts can always advertise.

The discount

It is always a puzzle as to why investment trusts sell at a discount to the underlying assets. This discount can be an advantage, or a disadvantage, or neither. If when you sell your shares in an investment trust, the discount has narrowed, then you would have gained. Note that this still does not mean that you would have made a profit - but that your loss might have been greater had the discount not narrowed. If the discount widens before you sell, then this would be a disadvantage. The discount is usually around 20%. If the discount gets too large (say, 50%), then a pension fund, for example, could easily buy up all the shares and wind up the trust, making a healthy profit for itself. No one can properly explain why this discount arises, other than that it is a result of demand and supply for the shares in the trust. Generally speaking, as the markets fall, the discount tends to widen, whereas as the market rises, the discount tends to narrow.

As an example, if an investment trust's share price stood at a 20% discount, you could buy £100 worth of underlying assets for £80. If the value of the investments rises, to, say, £110, this does *not* necessarily mean you are £10 better off, as it also depends on what has happened to the discount. If the discount has *fallen*, you will be *more* than £10 better off. However, if the discount has widened you will have benefited by less than £10. A summary appears in the table below:

	Initial purchase	Discount falls	Discount rises
Value of underlying investment	£100	£110	£110
Discount	20%	15%	25%
Price of share	£80	£93.50	£82.50
Your profit	–	£13.50	£2.50

As this example shows, you are running *two* risks with an investment trust share; the risk of the asset values owned by the trust, *and* the risk that the discount widens. With a unit trust you only have the first risk.

Other matters

There are around 200 investment trusts in existence. The Association of Investment Trust Companies, at Park House, 6th Floor, 16 Finsbury Circus, London EC2M 7JJ, provides much information about investment trusts and divides the trusts into twelve categories. These range from capital and income growth, through to smaller companies and special features. Each month they publish a list of the trusts showing a considerable amount of detail including the price, five year record, amount borrowed etc.

Limited life trusts

These trusts have a fixed redemption date, or a series of dates, and overcome the problem of the discount. The sooner the trust is to be wound up, the less the discount will be.

Split capital trusts

These trusts split their shares into two sorts - an income share for the investor who may not pay tax (eg charities, pension funds, individuals), and a capital growth share for the higher rate tax payer who is looking for growth, and not income. The income goes to the income shareholders, but the capital growth goes to the capital growth shareholders. Unlike ordinary investment trusts, all split-level ones have a redemption date. The income shares can stand at a premium to the fixed price at which they will be redeemed. The size of the premium is dependent on interest rate levels - the capital shares usually sell at a discount to the underlying asset, though this narrows as the redemption date gets nearer. Capital shares do not have a fixed redemption price since their value will depend on the market value of the underlying shares in the portfolio at the redemption date, whereas income shares have a fixed redemption price.

Investment trust warrants

There are over 30 investment trusts which have warrants attached to them. A warrant is not a share, but is another word for an option, ie a right to buy a particular share at a fixed price on a particular date (or range of dates) in the future. For example, ABC Investment Trust shares may be selling at £1, with its warrants selling at 20p on an exercise price of 85p. In other words, if you bought a warrant for 20p, it gives you the right to buy a share in the ABC Investment Trust at 85p. Thus the price of the ABC Trust share would have to exceed £1.05p before you made a profit. Usually the warrants are exercisable only once a year, though you can of course sell the warrant itself at any time on the stock market. Warrants are often granted by trusts as a sweetener when making a new issue, to compensate for the trust's shares going at a discount to the issue price when they begin to be traded on the Stock Exchange.

Blackstone Franks' verdict

This is a rather specialised form of investment, and has not grown nearly as quickly as unit trusts. The discount is puzzling, and makes it difficult to justify investing in a new investment trust.

Investment trusts have similar tax advantages to unit trusts, since both are exempt from tax on their own gains. Also, they both spread their risks over many investments, though investment trusts can invest in a wider range. However, they do have an additional risk over unit trusts, which is that the discount can increase and reduce the value of your shares. Investment trust warrants are very risky and are to be avoided.

K

KRUGERRANDS £

A coin which has a gold content. An investment in Krugerrands is really an investment in gold - *see* separate section. To avoid VAT, it is better to buy the coins offshore and keep them stored in an offshore bank. A South African Krugerrand has a gold content of about 91.6%. The coins come in 1 oz, ½, ¼ and $\frac{1}{10}$ oz sizes. You can buy them from a wide network of sellers including most branches of clearing banks and coin dealers, like Spinks.

Blackstone Franks' verdict
Risky. *See* comments on gold.

L

LEASING EQUIPMENT XXX

The *lessor* buys the asset, and leases (or rents) it to the *lessee*. The *lessee* does not own the asset, and pays a rent to the *lessor*. Leasing equipment to a qualifying lessee used to create massive tax deductions (called 'first year capital allowances') but those days are now over. The industry has been marred by several frauds, especially in the container market. There are no longer any significant taxation advantages, and there are growing risks over the 'residual value' (second-hand value) of equipment when the lease period ends, especially if the equipment is a computer.

Container leasing has a particularly bad name with investors. There have been at least two frauds by container leasing companies. It is a risky business as there can be no solid guarantee that the containers will be leased out all of the time, whatever may be claimed by the promoters. It is a high risk business.

Blackstone Franks' verdict
A useful method of obtaining off balance sheet financing for a business, but as an investment this is strictly for the professionals. Too risky for the dabblers.

LIFE ASSURANCE £££

Life assurance companies are very sophisticated and now provide:

1. Protection in the form of life cover.
2. Lump sum investments - annuities, investment bonds, income and growth bonds.
3. Regular savings investments - endowment policies, unit-linked savings plan.

(*See* separate sections covering 2 and 3.)

Protection in form of life cover
Life assurance for protection is relatively cheap. Although there are some policies which are a mixture of life assurance and investment (eg whole life policies and unit-linked savings plans), better results

are usually achieved if life assurance and investments are treated separately.

The two main types of protection policies are:

1. Term life assurance - *see* separate section.
2. Whole life assurance - *see* separate section.

Each of these kinds of policies can be subdivided into cover on:

(i) a single life
(ii) joint lives payable on first death
(iii) joint lives payable on second death

Blackstone Franks' verdict
Life assurance usually has a place to play in most people's personal financial planning. Read each of the individual sections to see which one might best suit you.

LIMITED EDITIONS XXX

A limited edition of porcelain, coins, or metal objects, can be sold in two ways. Either the number to be sold is specified at the outset, or the number sold is the number ordered or bought by a certain date. In the second method, the number to be sold is only known after you have agreed to buy.

With many limited editions there is unlikely to be a big demand. There have also been some rascals in this business who mislead the investor.

Blackstone Franks' verdict
Very risky - not to be recommended.

LLOYD'S UNDERWRITERS ?

A member of Lloyd's is known as a *name*. Names are grouped into syndicates to undertake insurance business earning a premium, but paying out if there are claims. Each syndicate usually accepts a particular type of insurance risk - marine, aviation, motor, etc. The risk for a name is *unlimited* - you can lose everything if your syndicate fails. The loss can be reduced by paying a 'stop loss' insurance premium whereby you are insured if your own losses exceed an agreed figure (ie your losses are stopped). A name can be a working name (who works full time at Lloyd's) or a non-working name.

In a well-run syndicate, the names can make spectacular returns, helped by some good tax breaks. However, there have been massive cases of fraud at Lloyd's, and some syndicates are badly run. A name can suffer heavy losses, or even face bankruptcy, as well as losing his or her original stake. Names in syndicates formerly run by PCW Underwriting Agency have been told they face losses of up to £250 million – in some cases over £1 million each. Figures for 1982 have been released (it takes three years to close accounts because only a small proportion of claims are usually settled in 12 months): in 1982, the net profit or loss per £10,000 share ranged from a profit of £14,476 (at Marine 728) to a loss of £22,500 (at Syndicate 895). Each syndicate has its own number, and there are about 400 of them. The average return in 1982 was between 1% and 11%, and 10 syndicates lost money for every 26 that made a profit.

There are some 28,500 names of whom over 5,000 work in the market as professional underwriters (the 'working names'). The rest (the 'non-working names') are inactive investors. Around 3,000 new names start each year, and large numbers retire. Application is open to anyone over 21 years old of any nationality.

You have to be wealthy to become a member, as the minimum asset figure which you must show is £100,000, although the members' deposits may be provided by a banker's guarantee.

There are various tax advantages to being a member of Lloyd's, including:

1. Underwriting profits are earned income.
2. The syndicate usually invests the premium income to produce capital gains for the names (taxed at 30%) instead of income (taxed at 60%). Often investments are made in capital gains tax-free British Government securities (called gilts).
3. There are especially extended delays allowed in paying your tax – which enables you to invest the tax money for further gains.
4. The use of the special reserve fund (to set aside funds for future underwriting losses against future claims) can be manipulated to avoid paying tax on today's income.
5. For inheritance tax purposes, the Lloyd's investment is reduced by 50% business property relief, and the tax is payable over 10 years.
6. Losses can be offset against all other income and even carried back against income for up to three years earlier.
7. For working names, especially favourable tax concessions apply on retirement annuity premiums paid against Lloyd's earnings.

Nomination

In order to become a name, you must be nominated by an underwriting agent and two sponsors who are already members. One of these must know you well, and one must be a director or partner of your proposed underwriting agent. You must show assets of at least £100,000 which are 'readily realisable'. Up to 40% can be in property other than your principal private residence. The rest can be listed securities or cash. Partnership assets, cars and livestock are not permissible, though antiques and artworks may be. Alternatively, Lloyd's will accept a bank guarantee or letter of credit which may be secured on some of the non-eligible assets. The bank would require substantial cover for the guarantee. Once accepted, the entrance fee is £3,000.

The deposit

In order to start underwriting, you must deposit with Lloyd's 25% (35% for overseas members) of the premium income to be underwritten. Traditionally, stocks and shares have been used, but it is increasingly popular to use a guarantee or letter of credit instead. The premium limit is twice your ready assets. All assets held by Lloyd's are registered in the name of Corporation of Lloyd's. Income from the deposit is paid out to the member. All assets tied up in the deposit (including those pledged to secure a bank guarantee) are eligible for business property relief for inheritance tax purposes up to the face value of the guarantee.

Your underwriting agent

Your agent is responsible for allotting your name to a syndicate with spare capacity. Most agents have between 20 and 50 syndicates at their disposal (there are about 400 syndicates in total). It usually takes three years to learn of the results, since claims can take a long time to be settled. That is why the taxman gives a three-year tax holiday on Lloyd's income - it takes that long to get the results.

Inheritance tax

The assets used in Lloyds to support the deposit are eligible for business property relief, which means that they are discounted by 50% in valuing them for inheritance tax calculations. This relief would be wasted if the Lloyd's underwriter leaves the asset to his or her spouse, unless the survivor also becomes a member of Lloyd's. It is therefore usually more sensible to leave such assets to other beneficiaries either directly or via a trust. For example, the assets could pass to a discretionary trust under which income and capital is paid to the beneficiary during his or her lifetime, but where the underlying assets do not form part of the estate for tax purposes.

Overseas members

An overseas member is also liable to UK tax because the income arises in the UK. To reduce the UK tax exposure, many overseas members obtain a bank guarantee on the deposit secured by offshore assets. Income from the offshore assets would be free of UK tax.

Blackstone Franks' verdict

Always take out a stop-loss policy and take specialist advice in deciding which syndicate to join. An excellent investment if you are in the right syndicate, but you can be made bankrupt if you're in the wrong one without a stop-loss policy.

LOCAL AUTHORITY LOANS £

The usual minimum investment is £500 or £1,000, and the rate of interest varies. Interest is usually paid out twice a year, and tax is deducted from the interest before it is paid to you.

Although local authorities are considered to be a relatively safe investment, we would caution investors - some may not turn out to be such a good investment if they overspend. To find out which local authority is offering the best rate, the Chartered Institute of Public Finance and Accountancy runs a loan bureau. They can be contacted at 532 Vauxhall Bridge Road, London SW1B 1AU (telephone 01-828 7855). Of course, a higher rate may reflect a greater risk.

Blackstone Franks' verdict
An illiquid loan. Some local authorities have been on the verge of bankruptcy.

LOCAL AUTHORITY STOCKS OR BONDS £

Local authority stocks (often called corporation loans or corporation stocks) are generally issued for fixed periods of six or more years. They work in the same way as most British Government stocks, except that you are liable for capital gains tax. Local authority bonds are often called yearling bonds because they commonly last for a year or so.

Local authority stocks
These are issued for a fixed period of six or more years, and some are undated (ie they have no fixed maturity date). They can be bought and sold on the Stock Exchange. If you sell the stock before it matures, you sell it on the Stock Exchange and you cannot be sure of the price which you will receive. As with British Government stocks, the return is a mixture of interest and capital gains. There is no minimum amount.

Local authority bonds - yearling bonds
These are usually for a fixed period of a year or two years. The minimum investment is usually £1,000, and you invest in multiples of £1,000. You can buy or sell them on the Stock Exchange. They are free of capital gains tax, but there is usually only a small prospect of making a capital gain as they are not issued at a discount.

Blackstone Franks' verdict
Yearling bonds are less volatile in price than local authority stocks,

and more liquid than local authority loans. These investments are reasonably safe. Note that all interest is paid after deducting basic rate tax, and higher rate taxpayers will have more tax to pay.

M

MANAGED OR MIXED FUNDS ££

A managed (or mixed) fund is one where the investment decisions are taken by the fund managers, and there is usually no specialisation. For example, a unit trust company might offer a Japanese unit trust (specialising in Japanese shares), or a smaller companies trust, or a managed fund (which allows the fund managers discretion to invest). Managed funds are usually offered in conjunction with most types of investments, eg unit trusts, endowment, investment bonds. A managed fund is not an investment in itself, but a choice within an investment – (*see* the separate sections on unit trusts, endowment policies, and investment bonds).

Blackstone Franks' verdict
Often a simple way out for the investor who is unsure of which fund to choose.

MAXIMUM INVESTMENT PLANS ££

A maximum investment plan is an endowment policy which is designed for investment, rather than life assurance. The life cover is minimal – sufficient for the policy to qualify for an endowment policy. Should death occur within the 10-year policy term, the greater of the guaranteed death benefit or value of the fund will be paid. Maximum investment plans are either unit-linked or with-profits. *See* the section on endowment policies for more details.

Blackstone Franks' verdict
See endowment policies.

MONEY MARKET ££

The money is dominated by the large banks and deals with overnight, weekly, monthly and yearly deposits of very large sums. The private investor can place large amounts on the money market to obtain a slightly higher rate of deposit interest over a period. The investment is usually equivalent to a large deposit account with a major bank.

The minimum money market deposit is usually about £10,000,

and can be invested either in a fixed account (similar to ordinary term deposit accounts with terms varying from over 1 to 5 years) or a notice account (the money is on deposit for an unlimited period, with a set period of notice for withdrawals of 7 days to 6 months).

The interest paid is usually calculated on a daily basis and credited at regular intervals, or at the end of the investment period if earlier. The rates payable reflect current money market interest rates, and can vary. Money market deposit accounts may be suitable for individuals with very large amounts as a short-term home until they commit their money on a longer-term basis. An example of this might be where a person intends to invest in unit trusts when he considers the time to be opportune.

Blackstone Franks' verdict

Good for a short-term investment, but not for a long-term one. For more details, *see* the section on bank deposits.

N

NATIONAL SAVINGS £££

There is a variety of national savings products, all run by the Government, and the interest rates on the whole are competitive with building societies, but as the certificates are tax-free they are very attractive to high rate taxpayers.

Below is a summary, and further details are given in the individual sections in this book (this information is available in National Savings leaflets).

	Max	Rate	Tax	Withdrawal notice
National savings certificate				
31st issue	£10,000	7.85%	None	8 working days
4th index-linked	£5,000	4.04% plus inflation	None	8 working days
Yearly plan	£200 per month	Fixed	None	14 working days
Other types				
National savings deposit bonds	£50,000	Variable	Paid gross but taxable	3 months
National savings investment accounts	£50,000	Variable	Paid gross but taxable	1 month
Premium bonds	£10,000	Prizes equate to 7.75%	None	8 working days
National savings income bonds	£100,000	Variable; can be indexed	Paid gross but taxable	3 months
National savings ordinary account	£10,000	Fixed	First £70 is tax free	Small amounts on demand; otherwise a few days

Blackstone Franks' verdict
See the individual sections.

NATIONAL SAVINGS CERTIFICATES £££

There are three kinds of national savings certificates:

1. Fixed, guaranteed return (now the 31st issue)
2. Index-linked
3. Yearly plan

All of the income is paid gross and is tax free, and they are very attractive to high rate taxpayers.

Fixed guaranteed return

The current issue is the 33rd issue. The interest rate improves over the five-year term of the certificate. If the certificates are encashed during their first year, the purchase price only is repaid. They can be purchased via the Post Office or banks. Repayments are free of all income tax and capital gains tax. A maximum holding is announced for each issue - it is £1,000 for the 33rd issue, although holders of previously matured issues can reinvest up to £5,000 in addition to up to £1,000 of the new issue. Husband and wife can own a maximum of £2,000. The tax-free compound annual rate of interest on the 33rd issue if held for five years is 7%. To earn 7% tax free, a 60% taxpayer would have to find a taxable product paying a grossed-up rate of 17.5%.

Index-linked

These certificates are linked to the monthly changes in the retail price index over five years. In addition, extra interest is earned - the longer the certificate is held the more interest is earned. The compound annual interest rate for the 4th issue is 4.04% in addition to inflation-proofing. These are also completely tax free. The maximum holding is £5,000 and is in addition to all other holdings of national savings certificates. If the certificates are cashed in before the first anniversary of purchase, only the sum invested is repaid. Cashing in early can be a disaster - the return after one year is only 6.01%.

Yearly plan

Monthly contributions of between £20 and £200 can be paid by a standing order. The interest rate is fixed from the first payment and interest is tax free. At the end of the year a certificate is issued for the value of payments and interest earned for the year. The certificate then earns a higher rate of interest than the monthly payments. The maximum guaranteed rate of interest is payable if the certificate is held for four full years. Details can be obtained from the Savings Certificate Office, Yearly Plan Section, Durham DH99 1NS.

Blackstone Franks' verdict

Good for higher rate taxpayers as the income is tax free. The 33rd issue pays 7% tax free, which for a higher rate taxpayer equates to a gross return of 17.5% before tax.

Very safe as British Government guaranteed, and can be index-linked. The collective total invested in, for example, building societies is £124 billion compared with £32 billion in national savings.

NATIONAL SAVINGS DEPOSIT BONDS £££

National savings deposit bonds are designed for people with lump sums to invest who are seeking capital growth. Interest is taxable but paid gross. There is a minimum holding of £100 and a maximum holding of £50,000. They are available to individuals, trusts, charities and all catagories of investors.

Interest is calculated on a daily basis starting from the date of purchase, and is added to the capital value on the anniversary of the purchase date. The rate of interest is varied from time to time to keep it competitive. The interest earned must be reported on your tax return.

Purchases can be made at most Post Offices, or through coupons in national advertising.

Repayment can be made on giving three months' notice. There are no penalties for repayment after the first anniversary of purchase. Repayment without notice is allowed on the death of an investor.

Blackstone Franks' verdict

Safe.

NATIONAL SAVINGS INVESTMENT ACCOUNTS ££

Up to £50,000 can be deposited in a national savings investment account. Interest is taxable, but no tax is deducted at source. One month's notice is required for withdrawals. Interest is earned on a daily basis, and credited to the bank book on 31 December each year. Application can be made at most Post Offices.

Blackstone Franks' verdict

Good way to start children saving as it needs only a minimum of £5 to open an account at any Post Office and the child is officially responsible for his own account once over the age of 7. Being taxable, not that attractive for taxpayers.

O

OFFSHORE FUNDS ££

Offshore funds usually mean funds which operate from a tax haven outside the UK. They are normally administered similarly to unit trusts, but they are not governed by the Department of Trade.

Offshore funds operate in a similar way to unit trusts with many of the same characteristics, eg full time professional management, wide investment spread, price of the shares being directly related to the value of the underlying assets, etc. If exchange controls were to be reintroduced, these investments might be affected.

Umbrella funds
(*See* separate section on Umbrella funds, which rank as **£££**.)

Offshore currency funds
These specialise in investing in foreign currencies, and there are two distinct types of funds available; a *managed currency fund* usually consists of a basket of currencies such as Deutschmark/ Yen/Sterling/Dollar/Swiss Franc etc, and the fund manager has discretion to move his investors' money among these currencies. *Multi-currency deposit funds* leave currency selection to the individual investor. Classes of shares in each of the five major currencies (and sometimes others) are offered. Switches are tax free.

Currency funds are subject to a tax charge on income which is explained below. On balance, the umbrella funds have more to offer.

Difference between offshore and onshore funds
An offshore fund is not liable to UK taxes on its income or capital gains, whereas an authorised onshore unit trust fund is only free of capital gains tax; the onshore fund still has to pay UK tax on income.

The Inland Revenue have introduced a nasty tax charge, however, to eliminate this difference. If an offshore fund distributes its income, then the UK taxman collects tax on the distribution. If, however, an offshore fund does not distribute at least 85% of the income, the taxman will charge any eventual gain you make on the units *not* to capital gains tax, but to income tax. Only those funds which distribute a minimum of 85% of income will receive the 'distributor status' from the Inland Revenue so that any gain is subject only to capital gains tax, as they are in a UK unit trust. However, if a fund loses distributor status (and the investor has no control over this) then the gain proceeds would be liable to income tax - a nasty shock for a 60% taxpayer.

Blackstone Franks' verdict
Offshore currency funds are of more limited use since the changes of 1 January 1984. They can be useful for non-domiciled UK residents or non-residents. Umbrella funds are rated very highly - see separate section.

OPTIONS ?

An option is the right to buy or sell an investment holding at a pre-agreed price at some time in the future. The option price simply represents the amount of money you have to pay in order to obtain the right to purchase, or sell, such an investment. For example, you might pay £10 to have to the right to purchase a share in a company for a fixed price of £100 within the next three months. If the price of that share increased to £125 within the three months, then you would exercise your right to purchase that share for £100. The cost of buying the share would be the price (£100) and the option price (£10), ie £110. However, the share itself is worth £125 at the time the option is exercised. If the price of the share fell, then you would not exercise your option, but you would have lost the £10 option price.

Options can be purchased for about 70 of the leading UK shares. A traded option is where the actual option contract acquires an intrinsic value and is traded in the market for value in its own right. Thus the option is bought and sold as if it were a share itself.

A *call* option grants the purchaser the right to *buy* shares from the seller (the seller is also known as the 'writer' of the option). A *put* option grants the purchaser the right to *sell* shares to the seller. In addition to those contracts based on quoted shares, there is a contract based on the Financial Times/Stock Exchange (FTSE) 100 Share Index, a contract based on £/US$, and one based on gilt edged stock.

Example of call option

	Price rises by 10p	Price falls by 10p
(a) Buy shares		
Price when bought	£1.00	£1.00
Price changes to	£1.10	£0.90
Profit or (Loss)	£0.10	(£0.10) Loss

(b) Buy call options

If the price for one share is £1.00, then 50p might buy a call option over, say, ten shares. This means the premium for the option is 5p or 5%.

	Price rises by 10p	Price falls by 10p
Number of shares	10	10
Price paid for call option	£0.50	£0.50
Price of share when option bought	£1.00	£1.00
Price of share changes to	£1.10	£0.90
Is option exercised?	yes	no
Profit or (Loss)	£0.50	(£0.50) Loss

Some option strategies

1. *Think price will rise?* If you think the price of a share will rise, then buy a call option. If you are right, you will make much more money than if you had bought the shares. If you are wrong, however, you will lose all your money, as the example below shows:

The profit is calculated by:

Value of ten shares	= 10 × £1.10 =	£11.00
Cost of ten shares	= 10 × £1.00 =	(£10.00)
less Cost of option		(£0.50)
Profit		£0.50

2. *Protection from share price fall?* If you own shares, and are worried about the price falling, the purchase of a put option can protect you.

Using similar figures as above: share price £1; you own 10 shares. Buy a put option costing 50p for 10 shares allowing you to 'put' the shares for a price of £1.

	Price rises by 10p	Price falls by 10p
You own 10 shares originally worth	£10.00	£10.00
Price changes to	£11.00	£ 9.00
Price of put option is	£ 0.50	£ 0.50
Your profit (loss) on the shares is	£ 1	nil*
But your net profit (loss) after accounting for the cost of the put option is	£ 0.50	(£ 0.50)

*your loss is nil, because you have bought the right to sell your shares (the put option) at a price of £1 *regardless* of how much the shares fall. Of course, if the share price doesn't fall, you will have paid the premium for the put option and have no income from it.

There are other more sophisticated (and complex) strategies which can be used.

Tax position
Overall, the options are liable to capital gains tax and the cost of an option can be treated as part of the cost of the shares, where the option is exercised. Where the option is not exercised, the writer has to pay capital gains tax on the premium, and the buyer can treat the premium as a loss for capital gains tax purposes. However, there is no real capital gains tax (or allowable loss) on options over UK gilts or qualifying corporate bonds.

Blackstone Franks' verdict
High risk, but high return. Not really an investment - a speculative gamble or hedge.

OVER THE COUNTER MARKET ?

More commonly known as the OTC, this market deals with stocks and shares outside the Stock Exchange. Although it is a very popular form of private investment in the United States, and well supported by a number of strong companies, the OTC market in the UK is still a young and weak market. However, there are signs that this may be changing as it becomes more respectable, and the Stock Exchange has now introduced a new division - the Third Market - to deal in OTC shares. At the moment shares quoted on the OTC tend to be those of weaker companies, and the market is not well regulated. There are about 200 companies quoted on the OTC.

(See also the section on the Stock Exchange.)

Blackstone Franks' verdict
A market yet to prove itself, but rapidly developing.

P

PENSIONS – COMPANY SCHEMES £££

The maximum pension benefits are shown below, including an example.

Maximum pension benefits

Example:	Man earning £24,000 pa
On retirement	
(a) *Pension* of ⅔ of final remuneration provided 10 years service:	£16,000 pa
(b) *Lump sum* of 1½ times final salary provided 20 years service (but pension reduced to 52% of final salary rather than 66.66%). This is subject to a limit of £150,000 (ie a final salary of £100,000).	£36,000
On death-in-service	
(a) Widow's pension ⅔ of maximum pension as if the husband had retired on grounds of incapacity instead of dying (⅔ × £16,000): Can be linked to RPI (retail price index)	£10,667 pa
(b) *Dependant's pension* together with widow's pension cannot exceed the amount of the member's pension (£16,000 less £10,667):	£5,363 pa
(c) *Lump sum* of four times final remuneration:	£96,000

On death after retirement
Same as death-in-service, but no lump sum.

Final remuneration

The most common definition of final remuneration is the remuneration for any one of the five years preceding the normal retirement date. Alternatively, this could be taken as the average of three or more years ending on the last day of the employment. In the case of directors who are able to control more than 20% of the voting rights of the company, benefits must be based on the average of the total emoluments for any three or more consecutive years ending not earlier than 10 years before the normal retirement date. In any case, the remuneration may be 'dynamised' which means that the remuneration may be increased to account for inflation. Benefits in kind, as shown on the PllD, may be taken into account where they are assessed to income tax.

Normal retirement date

The normal retirement age is no earlier than 60 for men and no earlier than 55 for women, except where a woman owns 20% of the company in which case the normal earliest retirement age is 60. Some occupations are allowed to retire earlier – footballers can retire at 35. An individual may continue to work after the normal retirement date, and if he elects to defer his benefits beyond the normal retirement date they may be increased.

Taxation position of pension fund

Pensions are extremely tax advantageous. All investment income and capital gains accumulate within the pension fund and are free of all UK tax. Any lump sums arising on death and at retirement are free of tax. Annual premiums paid into the fund are allowable as a deduction for corporation tax purposes. However, the contribution is given as a deduction only in the year in which they are *paid*. The contributions are not taxable as a benefit in kind of the individual. Special contributions, which are contributions other than the usual annual contributions, made by the company to purchase additional benefits for a member, may have to be spread over several years for corporation tax purposes. The amount allowed in a single year by special contribution is the greater of (a) £10,000 or (b) the amount of the annual contribution. For this purpose, the annual contribution is the total amount paid by the company in respect of all members to all schemes and not that relating just to the member or scheme concerned. Where the special contribution exceeds the amount stated above, it must be spread by dividing the contribution by the greater of £10,000 or the amount of the annual contribution, subject to a maximum of five years.

Contributions by an individual of up to 15% of annual remuneration are treated as an expense against remuneration.

Tax deductions obtainable

Apart from retirement planning, the scheme is providing deductions to reduce a company's corporation tax liabilities. Note that the payment must be made in the accounting year. Payment would also reduce the value of the shares in the company for both capital gains tax and inheritance tax purposes. Pensions can also be provided for wives. For the smaller company, the self-administered scheme (*see* separate section) can be even more advantageous.

Maximising benefits

In order to maximise the benefits, the amount treated as final remuneration should be as high as possible and the pension contributions paid should be as large as possible without overfunding. By dynamising past salaries, the benefits can be substantially increased. By arranging for the normal retirement age to be the earliest allowed, the contributions can be maximised. Funding for retirement pensions to escalate by the maximum permitted of 8½ per annum, maximising all death-in-service benefits and employing wives and setting up pensions for them, can all lead to increasing the amounts which can be paid tax deductible into the pension fund.

Additional voluntary contributions (AVCs)

As mentioned above, you can pay a further 15% of your remuneration into the fund and obtain full tax relief at your highest rate. These extra payments are known as AVCs (Additional Voluntary Contributions). This would be worth doing if the benefits offered by the pension scheme are low or the pension scheme has been introduced late in the individual's working life.

From October 1987, any employee who is a member of a company pension scheme will be able to set up his or her own AVC with *any* of the pension players – banks, building societies and unit trusts as well as life companies. Under the 1987 Budget, employees will no longer have to commit themselves to making contributions for at least five years. Now, they can pay on a yearly basis, with the ability to stop and restart payments at the beginning of the year. In addition, the payment will be allowed to be made net of basic rate tax, like MIRAS (which is the way mortgages are paid), with higher rate tax relief given through the PAYE coding. The Inland Revenue will continue to limit an employee to one AVC policy a year, but there is nothing to stop the employee making a fresh arrangement every year. Thus the employee can build up a portfolio of AVCs.

There is one major restriction. AVCs can only be used for pensions, not for commutation to a tax-free lump sum. This kills off the ability to use AVCs to guard mortgages (since the mortgage is supposed to be repaid by the lump sum received on retirement).

In addition, the employees' overall benefit from the company pension, together with the AVC pension, must not exceed the existing limit of two-thirds of final salary. Since the AVC operates on a money purchase basis, an employee paying high contributions and getting an excellent investment performance could find that the benefits have exceeded this limit. In such cases, the company benefit is cut back, so that the investor loses some of the contribution and could be hit for a tax repayment bill.

Insured schemes
An insured scheme is one which is run by an insurance company. The alternative is a self-administered scheme, which is covered in a separate section of this book.

The main types of insured schemes are as follows:

1. With-profits – the pension fund is increased each year by the declaration of bonuses which, once declared, cannot be taken away. (Oddly these are known as 'reversionary' bonuses.)
2. Non-profit – this type of scheme has a guaranteed benefit. It is not normally recommended unless there is a short period to retirement.
3. Unit-linked investment in units of various types of investment. Can be capable of producing very good results.
4. Deposit administration – this is a guaranteed cash deposit fund, but shows slow annual growth and cannot depreciate.

It is now normal practice in the case of all types of insured schemes for an open market option to be available without penalty. This means that the full value of the member's benefit is made available to purchase a pension from an insurance company other than that with which the pension scheme was effected. Therefore the individual can obtain several quotations at retirement from leading life assurance companies and arrange for his pension benefits to be taken with the company of his choice.

Most of the above has been written on the basis of a *money purchase* scheme (where the final benefits are based on the amount of the pension fund at retirement) which is the type normally effected for individual arrangements for directors. Medium or large group schemes are often *final pay* schemes in which the level of pension to be paid is by reference to final salary and number of years service, and is paid regardless of how well the underlying investments have performed. Here the employer may have to pick up the tab by increasing the company contributions if the investments have not performed well.

Blackstone Franks' verdict
Because of the generous tax concessions, pensions are an excellent form of investment. (*See* also pensions – self-administered schemes, and pensions – self-employed schemes.)

PENSIONS – SELF-ADMINISTERED SCHEMES £££

In a conventional pension arrangement monies are passed over to an insurance company which invests them. The company paying over the premiums cannot control the investments made by the insurance company.

Things are different with a small self-administered scheme. Here, the company setting up the scheme can also choose how the investments are made. A 'small' scheme is one with less than 12 members. Up to one half of the assets in the pension fund may be reinvested into the company by loans. Up to 12 employees or directors of the company can be part of the scheme. A company can only have one self-administered scheme. The funds could be used to purchase a property which is let, at market rent, to the company. The Inland Revenue's office in charge of the pension schemes (the Superannuation Funds Office) has to approve all such schemes. The monies cannot be used to make loans to the individual members, nor to purchase non-income producing assets such as yachts, paintings, etc.

Insurance companies who promote self-administered schemes often require 50% of the fund to be invested in the insurance company's own managed funds. These are known as hybrid schemes (part insured, part self-administered). This tends to diminish the self-invested administered character of the scheme, but can save costs.

A small self-administered scheme will only obtain the Superannuation Funds Office approval if it has a pensioneer trustee, who is an experienced pensions professional. The pensioneer trustee is not a watchdog for the Inland Revenue, but is there to ensure the rules governing such schemes are complied with.

Blackstone Franks' verdict

For the smaller, family controlled company, this is the ideal route. Monies paid into the pension fund are tax deductible, yet the company can re-borrow part of the funds for cash flow purposes. Any loans made to the company should be properly secured to protect the owners' pension funds. The minimum annual contribution should be about £10,000 to make the scheme cost effective. The disadvantage is the administration of the pension scheme, except where the scheme is administered by an insurance company via a hybrid arrangement.

PENSIONS – SELF-EMPLOYED £££

A pension plan for the self employed (known as retirement annuities) is a pension scheme run by an insurance company for individuals who are either self-employed or in a job where they do not belong to the firm's pension scheme. You pay a premium to the insurance company each year, which is invested by them and, when you retire, it pays you a lump sum and a pension for life.

Up to certain limits, all of the premiums are fully tax deductible. The insurance company does not have to pay tax on the profits it makes investing your money, and consequently pensions produce excellent returns. In addition, part of the fund at retirement may be taken as tax-free cash. Once you have handed your money over you cannot normally get it back until you are 60, at the earliest.

Depending on the plan, regular payments are not absolutely necessary. You could make payments as and when you can afford it.

There are over 100 different personal pension plans available. The main variations are:

1. how the pension is calculated
2. your choice of investment
3. how often you pay premiums
4. whether the plan allows you to borrow money back

The amount that is tax deductible depends on your earnings for the past six years. Having calculated that amount, it is fully tax deductible against earned and unearned income. There is a special list approved by the Inland Revenue of occupations where you can retire early and have a pension, eg acrobats, singers, deep sea divers, newscasters.

Life assurance may be provided under these pension arrangements and the premiums are fully tax deductible (within generous limits).

Widows' and dependants' pensions may also be provided. Contributions to these pension plans may continue even if you suffer from long-term incapacity, by a 'waiver of premium' benefit: in effect, contributions may be paid on your behalf up to the normal retirement age even though you have stopped earning due to incapacity.

Blackstone Franks' verdict
Pensions are an excellent investment because of the generous tax concessions.

PERMANENT HEALTH INSURANCE (PHI) £££

(*See also* personal accident and sickness insurance, hospital insurance, and private medical insurance.)

Male workers are seven times more likely to be away from work for more than six months than they are to die. The insurance which can soften the blow of long-term illness or disability is misleadingly called *permanent health insurance.* It offers nothing of the sort, but once you sign up, the insurance company is bound to keep you on the books, however sickly you become.

PHI provides a replacement income up to pension age to substitute income lost through prolonged sickness or disability –

which is often defined as 'unable to perform any part of normal duties'. Payments start after a deferred period of a minimum of four weeks, but this is more likely to be at least 13 weeks. The premiums are reduced if the deferred period is extended. The premiums depend on occupation, the age of entry, whether you are male or female, and the deferment period, and are fixed once the contract is in force. The maximum benefit payable is normally 75% of salary (less a single person's basic national insurance invalidity pension). Benefits are tax free up to the end of the first complete tax year; thereafter they are classed as unearned income. This should not be confused with sickness and accident insurance where the benefits are paid out after 8 days, are tax free, only last for 104 weeks, and premiums may be increased each year although renewal can be refused if disability has occurred.

The contract cannot be cancelled by the insurance company, neither can it refuse to renew the contract if your health deteriorates. Note that different companies can have different definitions of disability - some are harsh, while others take a more lenient approach. Policies are usually written to the age of 60 or 65 and benefits will cease at that age even if the disability continues. The level of insured benefits can either remain constant or increase in line with the RPI (retail price index) or by a fixed percentage.

A comparison of rates:

Annual premium (£) to provide £100 a week (£433.30 a month) exclusive of policy fee, inclusive of waiver of premium for male life - deferred period four weeks

Company	Policy written to age 60 Age next birthday at entry 30	40	50	Policy written to age 65 Age next birthday at entry 30	40	50	Annual policy fee
Abbey Life	87.63	147.92	357.42	108.54	185.12	397.10	14.40
Allied Dunbar	96.90	148.60	233.60	112.90	178.40	291.20	27.00
Canada Life	129.56	179.39	271.07	145.50	208.29	327.88	5.00
Cannon	-	-	-	138.66	199.32	307.64	6.00
Commercial Union	126.01	177.14	264.26	146.02	212.36	327.96	10.00
Confederation Life	104.86	143.86	272.98	128.26	189.79	402.97	10.00
Continental Life	175.92	280.44	459.78	203.22	351.31	628.42	24.00
Crusader	104.01	146.11	210.50	128.78	197.13	326.90	8.00
Eagle Star	110.00	160.00	235.00	140.00	200.00	310.00	10.00
Friends' Provident	101.27	151.32	256.08	118.73	187.40	332.90	10.00
FS Assurance	117.56	160.63	246.77	135.02	188.57	286.34	11.64
General Accident Life	103.80	147.90	259.50	129.60	191.70	336.20	10.00
GRE	134.80	172.30	259.80	156.30	219.30	330.30	13.80
Medical Sickness	88.00	119.00	172.00	102.00	141.00	213.00	6.00
Norwich Union	99.45	139.45	205.74	120.00	171.45	269.75	10.00
Permanent Insurance	98.00	132.00	191.00	113.00	157.00	237.00	6.00
Prudential	106.29	147.63	240.76	124.70	178.31	286.16	15.00
Royal London Mutual	114.50	167.50	263.00	130.50	197.00	321.00	18.00
Tunbridge Wells Equitable FS	-	-	-	332.64	367.44	446.64	Nil
TW Equitable	-	-	-	149.16	212.52	327.36	6.00
Zurich Life	97.86	133.98	196.89	109.51	156.11	238.83	8.16

Source: Planned Savings

Note that the above premiums would be reduced by about 50% if the policy was to pay benefits after 6 months rather than 4 weeks.

For women Women are generally charged 1½ times the male rates, as records show that they claim more often than men do. Some companies treat women more fairly. The Pru only adds one third; Tunbridge Wells Friendly Society and London Life add 25%; Norwich Union reduces the loading if the deferment period is increased. Many companies do not offer PHI to housewives, though Abbey Life, Commercial Union, General Accident, M & G Life, Norwich Union, Permanent Insurance, the Phoenix and Tunbridge Wells do offer such cover.

Deferment periods On average, the deferment periods chosen by most people are:

	% choosing
1 month	20
3 months	49
6 months	2
12 months	6

Blackstone Franks' verdict
A must for anybody who does not have a sizeable capital sum to fall back on.

PERSONAL ACCIDENT AND SICKNESS INSURANCE
££

(*See also* permanent health insurance, hospital insurance and private medical insurance.)

This contract insures you against accident or sickness, the benefits being in the form of either a lump sum or an income. The payments are made following death, loss of sight or a limb, or on permanent total disability. Unfortunately the contract is of an annual nature and subject to your state of health at the beginning of each year and can therefore be cancelled by the insurance company, unlike permanent health insurance which is non-cancellable. Any lump sum paid is usually free of tax, but income benefits are treated similarly to those from permanent health insurance policies, ie they are tax free until they have been received for one complete tax year.

Blackstone Franks' verdict
Because these policies can be cancelled, they are not as good as PHI (permanent health insurance).

PERSONAL EQUITY PLAN (PEP) £££

The personal equity plan (PEP) will allow individuals who are UK resident and ordinarily resident for tax purposes to hold shares free of both capital gains tax and income tax provided certain rules are adhered to.

The basic details of the scheme, which commenced on 1 January 1987, are as follows:

1. The investor must be an individual aged 18 years and over.
2. The maximum investment will be £2,400 per calendar year for each individual. Husband and wife can have a PEP of £2,400 each for a total of £4,800 per year. It is not possible to spread the £2,400 over more than one plan manager.
3. Funds held within a PEP may only be invested in ordinary shares quoted on a UK Stock Exchange or dealt in on the Unlisted Securities Market. A maximum of £420 per year (or 25% of the total PEP investment if larger) can be invested in unit or investment trusts.
4. The plans must be administered by an 'authorised PEP manager'. All dividends and interest must be reinvested in the PEP.
5. Authorised PEP managers may include stockbrokers, members of FIMBRA, licensed dealers in securities and a number of banks and other financial institutions.
6. To obtain the tax-free status for capital gains tax on realised gains and income tax on reinvested income, it will be necessary for the monies to be held within the PEP for more than one complete calendar year. For example, an investment made in January 1987 must be retained at least until January 1989 whereas an investment in December 1987 must also be retained until January 1989. This rule does not require that the original shares be held throughout the qualifying period, as shareholdings may be switched in the usual way without a tax charge.
7. Monies can be withdrawn at earlier dates but the tax reliefs would be lost.
8. There is no requirement to report either the acquisition or disposal of a qualifying PEP to the Inland Revenue.
9. Switching within the PEP is freely allowable. There is only one important restriction. Unit trusts can be sold and the proceeds reinvested in other unit trusts or shares. However, the proceeds of share sales cannot be used to invest in unit trusts or investment trusts. Thus switching out of unit trusts or investment trusts can only be a one-way process.

There are other information requirements:

(i) All PEP holders must be sent annual company reports on all the investments held under their plan. This will cause some administrative headaches for the plan managers.

(ii) Detailed statements must be provided to PEP holders under the PEP legislation at least annually. However, the Securities and Investments Board Draft Requirements go much further and are likely to require quarterly statements for the majority of PEP investors.

(iii) PEP holders must be given the opportunity to attend AGMs and vote if they so wish, although an extra charge can be made for this if required.

(iv) A report must be made to the Inland Revenue by the plan manager if the plan is surrendered or voided earlier than the mature phase.

Finally, it should be noted that personal equity plans can only be taken out with approved plan managers - thus individuals cannot set up their own plan. A plan manager must:

1. be approved by the Inland Revenue;
2. keep the records - and they are extensive - required by the Inland Revenue, including a full record of planholders referenced either by their national insurance numbers or tax district references;
3. keep a full record of all sale and purchase transactions for individual investors for up to five years; and
4. receive all dividends, unit trust distributions and deposit interest on behalf of PEP investors, reclaim the tax credit on dividends, and unit trust distributions, and hold the investments of the plan.

PEPs - are they worth it?

The table below compares PEPs with other investments, using certain assumptions as shown. The PEP easily outperforms a building society investment. It is also a clear winner over direct purchases of shares for high rate, though perhaps less conclusive for basic rate, taxpayers. However, even for the basic rate taxpayer the PEP avoids all reporting to the Inland Revenue (whereas each purchase and sale of a share must be fully reported) and nobody would be interested in providing him or her with a diversified share portfolio for a mere £2,400. So PEPs are a simple way of investing.

An additional important benefit for the PEP is the flexibility of being able to make tax-free withdrawals regularly to provide an income once the plan has matured. This is particularly attractive for older people requiring regular income.

To obtain £1,000 net income from an investment yielding 4% requires the following capital sums:

From PEP	£25,000
From stock market	
(a) High rate taxpayer	£62,500
(b) Basic rate taxpayer	£35,211

This illustrates the attraction of the PEP.

PEPs compared with other investments
Original investment: £2,400

	Value £	Growth %
For High Rate Taxpayers		
PEP	17,977	649
Direct investment:		
no CGT	14,743	514
with CGT	11,756	390
Building society	3,268	36
For basic rate taxpayers		
PEP	17,977	649
Direct investment:		
no CGT	17,043	610
with CGT	13,398	458
Building society	5,801	142

Assumptions:
1. PEP based on FT All-share, net of all charges on Save & Prosper's PEP
2. Building society based on a typical investment share account
3. Direct investment based on ten stocks performing on FT All-share, net of brokerage of £15 plus VAT per transaction.
4. Capital gains tax after indexation and £6,300 allowance.

Other uses of PEPs
PEPs can also be used to make provision for school fees, and for loan repayments, and we expect to see more schemes linked to this in the future. They are also a convenient method of building up an investment in the parent's or grandparent's name on behalf of a child, which can then be transferred to the child's own ownership at age 18.

Early surrenders
If you liquidate your PEP early there are no penalties (as is the case when an insurance policy is surrendered before maturity) but you lose the tax benefits.

Should you wait?
If you wait to invest until December, the qualification period is shortest. However, it means you have lost time to accumulate the largest tax-free fund. It only makes sense to wait until December if you think the stock market will fall in that period.

It should be noted that these plans allow the husband and wife each to invest, thus increasing the maximum investment to £4,800 per calendar year. Children over 18 can also invest in a PEP.

Main PEPs available

Plan manager	PEP type	Min investment (£)		Charges			Early withdrawal (£)	Shareholder information	Unit trusts	Shares in portfolio
		Lump sum	Monthly	Initial	Annual	Dealing				
Abbey National	Discretionary	420	35	5%	1.25%	0.5%	None	£20 per request	Fidelity Growth Income	5–8 equities
Bank of Scotland	Discretionary	1,000	40	–	1%	0.25%	20	£5 per arrangement	–	25% trusts 3 equities
	Discretionary	1,800	150	–	1%	0.25%	20	–	–	At least 5 equities
	Unit trust	120	20	3%	UT charge +0.75%	–	20	–	Scottish Income Fund or Standard Income	
Barclays	Discretionary	500	40	£25 up to £1,200; £40 above	£15 up to £1,200 £25 above	As incurred	20 per 1,000	None	–	Income or capital
	Unit trust	–	20	5%	0.75%	–			Barclays Unicorn General	–
Bradford & Bingley	Discretionary	600	50	5%	1.5%	None	None	£50	–	Blue chip companies
Brown Shipley/ Heseltine Moss	Discretionary	500	–	£30	1.25%	None	1.5% of value	None	BS unit trusts	–
Charterhouse/	Discretionary	421	35	£23	1.5%	1.5%	25	£25 per request	–	–
Royal Bank of Scotland	Unit trust	–	35	3%	1%	–	25		–	–

Plan manager	PEP type	Min investment (£) Lump sum	Monthly	Charges (%) Initial	Annual	Dealing	Early withdrawal (£)	Shareholder information	Unit trusts	Shares in portfolio
Commercial Union	Discretionary	1,000	35	£10	2.25%	0.75%	20 per 1,000	£15 per request +50 rise in annual charge	CU unit trusts	Blue chip companies
Equitable Life	Discretionary	1,200	100	–	2.5%	As incurred	None	As incurred	–	20 equities
	Unit trust	–	35	5%	0.5%	–	None	As incurred	Equitable Pelican	–
Fidelity	Discretionary	1,000	75	5%	1.25%	0.5%	None	£20 per request	Fidelity Growth & Income	5–8 equities
	Unit trust	420	35	5%	1.25%	–	None	–	Fidelity Growth & Income	–
Framlington	Unit trust	420	–	5%	1%	–	None	–	PEP 87	Growth portfolio of 30–40 equities
FS	Discretionary	2,400	–	5%	2.4%	–	50	£120	FS Balanced Growth Fund	5–10 equities
Gartmore	Discretionary	1,000	100	5%	1.25%	0.5%	25	£45 pa	Gartmore Global Fund	4 blue chips
GT*	Discretionary	2,400	–	£75	1%	As incured	None	n/a	GT International	Up to 8 equities

Plan manager	PEP type	Min investment (£) Lump sum	Monthly	Charges (%) Initial	Annual	Dealing	Early withdrawal (£)	Shareholder information	Unit trusts	Shares in portfolio
Hill Samuel	Discretionary	2,400	50	5%	1.5%	None	25	–	–	Growth portfolio or British Industry Fund
	Unit trust	–	20	5%	1.5%	–	25	–	HS income trust	–
Lamont	Discretionary	1,000	50	1%	As incurred	None	None	–	–	Blue chip or speculative portfolios
Lloyds	Discretionary	300	25	1% (£10 min)	1% (£10 min)	0.2%	None	£5 per request	–	Lloyds unit trusts and shares from list of 30
	Non-discretionary	300	25	1% (£10 min)	1% (£10 min)	1.5%	None	£5 per request	–	Selected from list of 30
Midland	Discretionary	240	20	5%	0.75%+ 1% on shares	–	–	–	Midland Unit Trust	–
MIM Britannia	Discretionary	1,000	50	5%	1.25%	0.2%	None	£35 pa	Choice of MIM trusts	Blue chip or special situations; 3–8 equities
	Unit trust	420	20	5%	1.25%	–	None	–	Choice of MIM trusts	
M & G*	Unit trust	420	35	5%	1%	–	None	–	Choice of M&G trusts	–

Plan manager	PEP type	Min investment (£) Lump sum	Monthly	Charges (%) Initial	Annual	Dealing	Early withdrawal (£)	Shareholder information	Unit trusts	Shares in portfolio
Natwest	Discretionary	450	36	-	2%	As incurred	25	None	-	3 blue chips
	Non-discretionary	1,200	-	£25	£10	As incurred	25	None	-	Select from list of 30; choices out-side list at £10 extra
	Unit trust	420	20	5%	0.75%	-	25	-	Country Income & Growth	-
NM Schroder	Discretionary	300	25	5%	1.25%	0.2%	None	£25 pa	NM Schroder Income Fund	Choice of trusts and up to 10 equities
	Non-discretionary	2,400	-	5%	1.25%	As incurred	None	£25 pa	-	One equity from a list of 30
Prudential	Discretionary	600	75	-	2%	As incurred	None	10% of plan value	Holborn Unit Trusts	One sixth in unit trust and 20 equities
	Unit trust	420	-	5%	1%	-	None	-	Holborn Unit Trusts	-
Save & Prosper	Discretionary	400	50	1.5%	1.25%	0.75%	25	£25 per request	-	Around 10 equities
	Non-discretionary	500	-	1.5%	1.25%	As incurred	25	£25 per request	-	Choose from a list of 70
	Unit trust	250	20	5%	1.25%	-	25	-	Choice of 28 trusts	-

Plan manager	PEP type	Min investment (£) Lump sum	Monthly	Charges (%) Initial	Annual	Dealing	Early withdrawal (£)	Shareholder information	Unit trusts	Shares in portfolio
Yorkshire Bank	Discretionary	200	20	–	1.5%	1%	Full year's charge	As incurred	–	–
	Non-discretionary	200	–	–	1.5%	1%		As incurred	–	Choose from list of 30
	Unit trust	200	20	3%	1.5%	–	–	–	S&P High Return	–

Blackstone Franks' verdict

A must for any investor in equities. A PEP plan can be set up for each member of the family over 18. The charges are not as important as the quality of the fund managers. For example, in the *Financial Times* of 28 February 1987, Fidelity were the leaders in the 'Great Investment Race', having converted £35,000 given to them 5 months earlier to £102,807! By mid-March it was over £135,000! Choice of good investment managers is crucial; comparison of costs is of secondary importance.

PREMIUM BONDS £

Instead of receiving interest on your money, a premium bond gives you a chance of winning a prize. The total value of all the prize money is equal to interest on all the bonds. The prize money is tax free. They can be purchased at most Post Offices and banks. You can cash in your premium bonds to get back their face value after eight clear working days' notice. The bonds are sold in units of £1, and the minimum purchase is £10. The maximum any one person can hold is £10,000. Premium bonds can only be held in the name of an individual, and not by an organisation. The highest prize is £250,000. The bond does not become eligible for prizes until it has been held for three clear calendar months following the month of purchase. Every prize winner is notified by post at the last address recorded at the Bonds and Stock Office, so it is important to keep them informed of any change of address. The prize fund represents about 7.75% of the total value of eligible bonds, which is received tax free.

Blackstone Franks' verdict

The interest return is clearly based on the luck of the draw, but the return of capital is guaranteed. In other words, it's a gamble where the stake money is always returned - but you may have lost the income from investing in an alternative medium.

PRIME RESIDENTIAL PROPERTY FUNDS £

Residential property funds invest in central London houses which are suitable for letting to wealthy individuals or company employees. There are three companies which offer a residential property fund - Hendersons, Schroders and Target. The houses are usually valued at more than £350,000. Existing unit trust regulations do not allow property funds, on the grounds that investments should be liquid and be confined primarily to investments in stocks and shares. Residential property funds are therefore structured as investment bonds. The disadvantage with investment bonds compared with unit trusts is that they are subject to capital gains tax within the fund.

There are also special problems with these residential funds. Because of the illiquid nature of the shares held, you may find it difficult to realise your investment in the event that everyone wants to switch out. However, so far these funds have had excellent results.

Blackstone Franks' verdict
If you want to invest in residential property in London, this is probably the simplest and easiest way to do it. A relatively safe home for your money.

PRIVATE MEDICAL PLANS ££

(*See also* permanent health insurance, personal accident and sickness insurance and hospital insurance.)

There are over 5 million people covered by private medical insurance. The purpose of these plans is to enable you to obtain certain medical treatment privately rather than through the National Health Service. This means that you can usually select the time you want the treatment, can select a hospital for your own convenience and even possibly choose a particular surgeon, obtain benefits such as a private room with television and telephone and more flexible visiting hours. Some policies provide a daily cash benefit to pay for incidental expenses while in hospital, such as telephone calls.

The main companies providing cover are BUPA, PPP, Western Provident Association (WPA), First Health, and Bristol Contributory Welfare Association (BCWA). These companies are constantly changing their premiums and policy terms. There are group plans available which can be cheaper. Payments into such plans are not tax deductible, and if your employer pays for them they will be a taxable benefit if you are a director or earn more than £8,500 pa.

The figures below show the relative costs of the four major health insurers, for a family with two children, where the oldest member is 42, and cover is up to the level of a London Postgraduate Teaching Hospital. These rates were as of November 1986.

Medical insurance costs per family – oldest member 42

	PPP	BUPA	WPA	BCWA
*Annual premium**	£836.40	£840.09	£717.00	£525.10
Maximum benefits pa	no limit	no limit	£45,000	£45,000
Benefits				
Hospital accommodation**	full refund	full refund for BUPA hospital	up to £195	up to £191

	PPP	BUPA	WPA	BCWA
Surgeons' and anaesthetists' fees:				
Major+	£650	£661	£665	£625
Major	£525	£538	£340	£515
Intermediate	£325	£306	£310	£310
Minor	£160	£156	£160	£155
Complex Major	full refund	£919 to 1,849	£1,300	£1,350
Operating theatre fees	full refund	full refund in BUPA participating hospitals	limits depending on operation	up to £2,000
Home nursing	£1,000 pa	£600 pa	full refund up to 26 weeks	full refund up to 13 weeks
Physician's services	£18 per day	up to £115 per week	up to £375 pa	up to £147 per week
Consultant physiotherapy outpatient	£270 pa	£375 pa	up to £375 pa	£375 pa
Cash benefit while NHS patient	£23 per day	£25 per day	£175 per week	£147 per week

*Includes discounts for annual payments by direct debit but not for group discounts
**Up to London NHS postgraduate teaching hospital levels

Outside London, cover would be cheaper. You could come unstuck, though, if you live outside London but become ill on a visit there, as you'd be insured for non-London rates but end up paying London prices.

BUPA is the giant of the private medical business with some 70% of the market. PPP is its nearest rival, with WPA and BCWA following some way behind.

The elderly

Remember that the policy is only an annual one – the insurers can refuse to renew your contract. BUPA, PPP and WPA will not take on new members over the age of 65. All three companies have age bands with different premiums, and the cost of cover can increase dramatically with advancing years. BCWA will allow new members to join up to the age of 69. PPP has a special Retirement Health Plan for which the upper age limit for joining is 75. It is limited to in-patient cover up to £4,500 per annum, or £9,000 in case of open heart surgery. It only comes into effect if there is a waiting list for a bed in an NHS hospital for more than six weeks, but this seems a reasonable compromise.

Discounts

You can often get discounts by paying by direct debit or by being a member of a group scheme or of a professional organisation. Company schemes usually offer excellent discounts.

Blackstone Franks' verdict
With the problems of the National Health Service, these schemes have become much more popular. About 30% of the people who use private medicine in the UK finance the costs out of their own pocket, and do not bother with insurance. Whether or not this is the right approach would depend on how much private medical treatment is required during your lifetime. On balance, we think it a useful insurance.

PROPERTY INVESTMENT £

Property investment includes holiday lettings, residential funds, farms and woodlands, which are each part of a separate section in this book.

Investing in your own home is discussed in a separate section in this book.

Investing directly in property requires some knowledge, a lot of time, and careful advice to avoid some of the tax pitfalls which surround property investments. It is a long-term investment, and can lead to considerable difficulties. For example, the Rent Acts and the Landlord and Tenant Acts are heavily weighted against landlords, and you might find that your investment in property does not produce the income which you anticipated. The problems of direct investment are best avoided by investing in some form of shares, unit trust, or investment bonds with a property fund. Investment direct into property is an illiquid one – it can take some time to sell a property.

London is the strongest rental market in the UK. Over 90% of renters stay for two years; perhaps 50% stay for a third year. Returns are not that high, and capital growth is needed to make the investment attractive. An unlet property means the investment is not producing an income. The cash flow might look like this:

Cash flow for a London rental – investment property

Taking a notional 3-bedroom flat in Central London valued at £200,000

	£
Property purchase price	200,000
Stamp duty	2,000
Solicitor's fees	1,000
Survey fee	350
Decoration and furnishing (normally allow up to 10% of the purchase costs)	20,000
Plus any agency acquisition fees	
Total investment	223,350

Potential rental, say, £380 a week	
Total annual rental (approx.)	19,000
Less	
Rental fees at 10%	1,900
VAT at 15%	285
Management fees at 5%	95
VAT at 15%	14
Tenancy agreement and stamp	50
Inventory fees	40
Ground rent (say)	15
Service charges (say)	800
General and water rates	750
Nominal repairs	200
Contents insurance	120
Total outgoings	4,269
Rental surplus (before financing costs)	14,731
Notional gross rental return	14,731
£223,350 = 6.6%	

Note that the returns shown are *before* interest costs

Blackstone Franks' verdict
Property can be a good 'home' for your money. There are, however, better and simpler media than direct property purchases.

Q

QUOTED SECURITIES ££

See Stock Exchange.

R

RACEHORSES ?

The rules regulating racing and syndicated ownership are made by the Jockey Club. Those governing syndicated ownership of horses which are to be raced state that no more than 12 persons may share an interest in a horse. Buying a share in a horse is known as buying a 'leg'. The syndicate must be registered with the Jockey Club. There are professional managers who will organise the syndicates.

A member of a syndicate will have to continue to make payments into the syndicate to cover the training, maintenance and running costs, unless of course the horse starts to make a profit. A one-twelfth share can often be had for as little as £15,000 plus about £700 a year for the cost of training and running the horse. It costs on average about £8,000 a year to own a horse. If the prize money exceeds the cost, you will receive a dividend. Prize money is tax free but at the same time, no relief is available for expenditure on training. Losses or profits made by racing and any increase in value due to its success are neither taxed nor allowed. If the horse is leased for racing, leasing receipts will be taxable.

Blackstone Franks' verdict
A risky investment, even for those who have studied form and know about horses. Buy a 'leg' for fun not for profit – this is a gamble not an investment; a racing uncertainty.

RETIREMENT ANNUITIES £££

See pensions – for self-employed.

S

SCHOOL FEES PLANNING ££

Introduction
About half a million children attend private schools, with fees per term ranging from £380 to £2,300. Private schooling costs have always been high, but a recent survey showed that families whose children were going to private schools were not necessarily high earners. About half of the parents had an income of less than £25,000 per annum, with some as low as £10,000.

Whichever method is used to fund school fees, the following matters should be taken into account:

1. The possibility of the child not going to private school.
2. The possibility of the child changing to a different school mid-stream.
3. Death or incapacity of the child.
4. Possible increase in cost due to inflation.
5. The possibility of abolition of private education.
6. Deterioration of the parents' financial circumstances.
7. Death of the parents.
8. Breakup of the marriage.

There are three major sources for funding school fees, and we analyse each of these below:

1. from capital
2. from income
3. other sources

From capital
You pay a lump sum to an insurance company or a broker or a school, and the money is invested in a variety of ways. Some schemes have some tax advantages (in particular the school fees composition schemes and educational trusts). The three main types of capital schemes are:

(a) School fees composition schemes
(b) Educational trusts
(c) Fixed interest schemes

(a) School fees composition schemes
You pay a lump sum to a school representing school fees paid in advance. The school then invests the money, usually in an annuity which starts paying out when the child goes to school. The amounts you have to invest will vary from school to school depending on the fee levels and the discount they might give you for paying in advance.

These schemes are essentially deferred annuity contracts. Because the school enjoys charitable status, its income is free of tax. The school pays the lump sum over to an insurance company in return for an annuity. The annuity, in the hands of the school, is tax free. The scheme is thus particularly attractive to a higher rate tax payer since he would not be liable to either income tax or capital gains tax arising from the investment of the lump sum by the school. If instead he purchased the annuity, there would be income tax to pay.

The size of the discount which the school is able to offer will largely depend on the length of the period before the fees become due and the level of interest rates at the time the lump sum is paid.

Advice should be taken on the inheritance tax position of the parent or any other relative who makes the lump sum payment.

One of the main advantages of the school fees composition schemes is that they are reasonably simple to formulate and convenient to operate. However, they can be very inflexible. For example, a repayment might be made if the child does not attend the school, but usually on very unattractive terms. Schemes vary as to what happens if the child leaves the school or dies before his education has been completed. A parent should also discuss the position if the advantages relating to educational charities are abolished in the future.

(b) Educational trusts
Educational trusts are designed to overcome some of the disadvantages of the school fees composition schemes, since they are independent versions of the composition fees schemes or created by the schools themselves. You can usually switch funds from the benefit of one child to the benefit of another (which may not be the case with school fees composition schemes), and you do not have to nominate the school to which the fees are to be paid until shortly before the child starts school. If the child should die before the end of the plan, the amount paid into the plan, less any school fees payments already made from the plan, is usually guaranteed to be repaid under the trust deed.

The tax advantages of the deferred annuity contract being paid to an educational trust are the same as for the school fees composition scheme, and this scheme is therefore attractive from this point of view.

(c) Fixed interest schemes
The lump sum is applied to purchase suitable fixed interest investments such as British Government stocks, local authority bonds and national savings certificates. It may also be possible to make use of any existing investments owned by the payer. The purpose of the scheme is to ensure that, as far as possible, the investments mature shortly before the necessary funds are required to pay the school fees.

These schemes are generally more flexible in that the investments are not restricted for educational purposes – the money can be used for anything else if circumstances change. However, it can take some time to work out a worthwhile scheme, and the income would be taxable.

From income
There are a number of different ways in which these schemes can be set up, but most involve saving regularly by taking out investment-type life insurance policies, ending year by year as the fees become due. Thus the payments are spread over a longer period than the period of education. The amount of monthly savings is obviously less if you start these policies earlier rather than later. The scheme should also include some insurance should the income provider die early, become disabled or be made redundant.

There are three main methods of school fees planning out of income:

(a) Life assurance schemes
(b) Unit trust regular savings plan
(c) Deferred annuities through an educational trust

(a) Life assurance schemes
These are essentially endowment policies – *see* separate section.

(b) Unit trust regular savings plan
These can either be straightforward unit-linked savings plans (*see* separate section), or they can represent direct investments into unit trusts on a regular (usually monthly) basis. In this latter case, no life cover is provided and consideration should be given to this separately. A unit trust savings plan provides greater flexibility than unit-linked savings plans since they may be terminated at any time without penalty. Capital gains tax on realisations and income tax on income would be payable.

(c) Deferred annuities through an educational trust
These are similar to a lump sum investment in an educational trust, except that rather than paying a lump sum to an educational trust, premiums are paid monthly. Each premium purchases a guaranteed

level of fees provided by way of a deferred annuity arranged through an educational trust.

Other sources

Apart from meeting the costs of school fees from your own capital or income, the following are other ways which may be open to parents:

(a) A deed of covenant – *see* separate section.
(b) Borrowing – you may be able to arrange a loan based on the security of your home or other investments or based on any investment type life insurance policies.
(c) If the parent is a partner in a trading partnership, it may be possible to arrange for a lump sum to be withdrawn from the partnership, but replenished by a bank loan. Tax relief might be obtained on such a loan.
(d) A loan could be made against pension funds.
(e) Setting up an accumulation and maintenance trust fund with grandparents' money (not the parents') has tax advantages. *See* section on trusts – accumulation and maintenance.
(f) As a last resort, capital might be released by moving to a cheaper house.

Blackstone Franks' verdict

School fees planning is usually more tax effective if a lump sum is invested, but it is also wise to ease the pain of paying school fees by funding over a number of years.

SECOND HOMES ?

A second home is not really an investment, since while it might appreciate in capital terms, it does not provide an income. (*See* the section on property investment.)

If you own two homes, and live in each, it is possible to elect which house will count as your tax-free house for capital gains tax purposes. This election must be made in writing within two years of the date you obtain both houses. If an election is not made, then the house in which you live most of the time will become the one which is tax free.

Blackstone Franks' verdict

As an investment, a second home can have problems. It can, however, give much pleasure.

SHARES ££

See Stock Exchange.

SHARE OPTION SCHEMES (APPROVED) £££

There are three kinds of share option scheme:

1. 1984 Finance Act schemes
2. Save-as-you-earn (SAYE) schemes
3. Profit-sharing schemes

A share option allows an employee to buy shares at a pre-set price (the 'exercise price') at some future time. If at that time the market value of the shares is greater than the exercise price, it is obviously attractive to take up the option. If on the other hand the market value is lower, there is no point in the employee exercising his or her option.

1984 Finance Act schemes

Provided that all the conditions are met, the only capital gains tax is payable on the gain. If the conditions are not met, the employee may face an income tax liability.

The main conditions which have to be met are:

1. The maximum value of the shares acquired for any participant is the higher of £100,000 or four times his or her earnings.
2. The exercise price must be the market value at the date when the option was *granted* (not, of course, the date the option is exercised).
3. The option cannot be exercised less than three years or more than 10 years after it is granted.
4. At the time the option is granted, a director must be full time (working at least 25 hours a week). Other employees are required to work at least 20 hours a week. The Inland Revenue do not require this condition to be met at the time the option is exercised, but companies usually take the share option away if the individual leaves.
5. The share option can be in any quoted company or in an unquoted company not controlled by any other company. It cannot be granted by any unquoted company controlled by another unquoted company (eg a subsidiary of an unquoted company).
6. The participant cannot own 10% or more of a close company. Shares owned by 'associates' (eg wives) would count in calculating the 10% limit.
7. The shares can be in an overseas company, or a non-trading company, or in a company eligible for BES (business expansion scheme).
8. The shares must be ordinary shares and fully paid up, but they do not have to be issued at the time the option is granted.
9. The shares could already be issued and owned by, say, a trust and the participant – on exercising the option – could receive those existing shares from a trust.

10. Although the options cannot be in shares of a subsidiary (unless the parent is a quoted company), the number of options granted can be linked to the performance of the subsidiary. Any such performance targets must be easily measurable (eg based on audited accounts) and not dependent on any subjective opinion of the directors.
11. The scheme does not have to be open to all directors or to all (or any) employees.

Takeovers
If the company is taken over, the options can prove to be a problem. The options granted under the approved scheme cannot be re-expressed in shares in the new parent or exchanged for options over such shares. Professional advice should be taken in these circumstances.

Save-as-you-earn (SAYE) schemes
This scheme differs greatly from the 1984 Finance Act scheme. It must be open to all full-time directors and employees who have been with the company for at least five years, and who are resident in the UK. The scheme must also be approved by the Inland Revenue.

Someone who participates in this kind of scheme must take out a five-year SAYE contract through a building society. At that time he will be granted an option to buy shares in the company, normally at 90% of the market value. The amount he or she must pay through the contract ranges from £10 to £100 a month.

At the end of the five-year period, the participant can use the proceeds of the contract (which may include a bonus equal to 14 monthly payments) to buy shares under the terms of the option.

The participant has two other choices. He can let the contract run for another two years without making any more payments and collect another bonus of the same amount and use the increased amount to buy shares; or, alternatively, he can keep the cash and not take up any shares.

As before, only capital gains tax is payable on the eventual disposal of the shares. Because of the small amounts involved, the gain may fall below the capital gains tax threshold.

Profit-sharing schemes
Another kind of plan which needs Revenue approval is the profit sharing scheme. Again, this must be open to all full-time directors and employees who have been with the company for at least five years. The scheme can be open to non-resident employees, but they may not have the same tax protection.

The company pays money into a trust which exists only to

acquire shares in the company on behalf of employees. All monies paid into the trust are tax deductible. The trust can buy shares either as newly issued ones (in which case, the money goes back into the company) or the shares are bought from existing shareholders.

Provided the shares are held on the employees' behalf in a special trust for at least five years, no income tax will have to be paid on their appropriation; if, however, the shares are disposed of earlier, some income tax may have to be paid. Any subsequent rise in the value of the shares between appropriation and disposal should be subject only to capital gains tax.

The maximum payable into the trust each year by the company is the higher of £1,250 per employee or 10 per cent of the P60 salaries of the employees, though in no case can the amount exceed £5,000 per employee.

These schemes can create a good market for the shares of the company without having to obtain a quote. The rules can force any employee who leaves the company to offer his shares back to the other shareholders.

Blackstone Franks' verdict

Get as many of these as you can! You don't have to exercise the option, and if you only exercise it where it's obvious you're onto a good thing (eg the company's going public, or there's a takeover), you can't lose. Note that you can only get share option schemes from your employer company.

SINGLE PREMIUM BONDS £££

See investment bonds.

STAMPS ?

There are a very large number of people throughout the world who collect stamps, and very rare stamps can fetch very high prices. However, stamp values can fall as well as rise. There have also been a few unscrupulous dealers who have sold overpriced portfolios. To invest seriously in stamps you should know a lot about them and study catalogues, go to auctions, join a philatelic society, and read relevant books. Very small differences in printing and water marks can affect price drastically. The condition of the stamp is vital. Unusually, even forgeries and printing errors can be worth more than the legitimate stamps. Buying special issues of commemorative stamps is unlikely to be a good investment because they are generally issued in very large quantities.

So condition, intensity of colour, whether used or mint, and plate numbers on early British stamps are prime factors that determine value. It is usually best to specialise if you are to collect stamps. Always ask for a certificate of authenticity, which is issued by either the British Philatelic Association or the Royal Philatelic Society. Remember that prices can crash, and have done so. In 1981, the 1928 Cyprus Anniversary of British Rule stamp sold for £750. In 1987, its value is £275.

Blackstone Franks' verdict
Risky – you really have to know what you are doing and spend a lot of time at it.

STOCK EXCHANGE ££

Shares in a company can provide an income (or dividends) and also might increase in price to give you a capital gain. However, share prices can also fall. It is difficult to choose the right share, and generally considered good to spread your risks. For ease of spreading your investments, read the sections on investment trusts, unit trusts, and investment bonds.

Unit trusts in particular have grown as a method of investment, as opposed to investing directly by individuals onto the stock market which has declined from just under 60% of all investors in 1963 to less than 25% today.

The Stock Exchange deals in:

British Government stocks
Local authority stocks and bonds
Full listing
Unlisted securities market (USM)

Apart from full listing, each of the above has a separate section in this book. Full listing is given to large public companies.

SEAQ stands for Stock Exchange Automated Quotations system and is an electronic price display and recording system. It carries information on 3,500 UK stocks (including USM) and gilts.

Shares on SEAQ are categorised as follows:

Alpha – the aristocracy of these categories. These 60 or so shares are the most actively traded. 'Market makers' (the new word for jobbers) display prices at which they are bound to deal. These shares are expected to have ten or more market makers. Alphas have two special features – trade details are published immediately and there is a running tally of trade volume.

Beta – the second rank of 500 shares which are often traded but not as frequently as front-line alphas. Firm dealing prices must be given. Betas have four or more market makers.

Gamma – less active shares. Prices are only an indication of actual dealing prices. Gammas are required to have at least two market makers. Most offerings on the USM fall into the gamma or delta class.

Delta - the lowest class of shares which trade infrequently. Deltas aren't even carried on SEAQ. Instead, the names of dealers are listed on another information system, TOPIC. No prices are given. Deltas may end up with just bargain matchers - if you want to buy, he scouts round for a seller, and vice versa.

Blackstone Franks' verdict

Investing in shares via unit trusts or investment bonds is a safer way of investing in the Stock Exchange. Local authority stocks and bonds, and British Government stocks, can have a part to play in an investment portfolio. Remember also Mark Twain's observation that October was a particularly dangerous month for speculating on the stock market. He went on to add that the other dangerous months are January, February, March, April, May, June, July, August, September, November and December ... However, investment in the Stock Exchange over the past 10 years has proven to be a good investment.

T

TERM LIFE ASSURANCE £££

See also whole life assurance.

Term assurance is one of the cheapest ways of insuring your life. It is called term insurance because its cover lasts for a fixed number of years. You choose how long. During that time you pay regular premiums; if you die, the policy pays out a fixed amount. If you survive to the end of the term, you get nothing back and stop paying premiums.

Term assurance provides worthwhile protection for your family during the years of peak financial vulnerability; that, is while the children are growing up. But it can also be used for other things: for example, you could take out a five-year policy to cover a large loan. If you were to die before repaying the loan, the term policy would take care of the outstanding amount. Longer term policies, say 25 years, are ideal for covering a mortgage.

Term assurance is also useful in planning for inheritance tax. For example, tax rules say that you can give away as much money as you like, but if you die within seven years of making such a gift, there might be tax to pay; a seven-year term policy could cover that possible inheritance tax liability. You can choose a policy which either (a) pays a lump sum or (b) pays an annual income. There are no surrender values or paid up values on term assurance policies. If premiums cease, the policy lapses, with the insurance company being under no further liability. Policies do not normally go beyond the age of 60 or 65.

A *level term* pays out a tax-free lump sum if you die before a fixed date (eg 20 years). If you don't die within that time, you get nothing, and all your premiums are kept by the insurance company. Useful for cover for the breadwinner, or linked to bank or other loans. The advantage is that you know exactly how much your family will get.

A *decreasing term* is the same as level term, except that the tax-free lump sum paid if you die decreases over the years – and hence such a policy is commonly used to pay off a mortgage or loan if you die, and is called a mortgage protection policy. Where the mortgage depends on joint incomes, two single life policies may be better than a joint life policy, especially if there are dependent children. It is also simpler should the marriage break up.

If the policy includes *family income benefit*, this means that there is a payment of a tax-free income to your dependants over the remainder of the term of the insurance. The income could be one which increases over those years. Some policies allow for some or all of this income to be paid as a lump sum. Family income benefit policies are particularly useful for a couple with children. The policy could be on joint lives with the benefit payable on first death. Because the cover declines over time, the premiums on these policies are much cheaper.

Finally, there are *flexible term policies* which can have various options such as enabling you to increase the amount of cover each year by a fixed amount (10% pa, say) or linked to the retail price index. The policy may be renewable, which allows you to renew the policy at the end of the term without a need for a medical check. A policy may allow you to convert it to another life policy, eg whole life or endowment, without the need for any further medical checks, which can be a very useful option. All three flexible options would make your policy increasable, renewable and convertible.

Examples of costs – life assurance

		Man aged 30, annual premium £	Woman aged 30, annual premium £
Level term			
	£100,000 lump sum	128.00	100.00
or	£15,000 annual income	136.50	117.00
Increasable, renewable			
	£50,000 initial lump sum increasable by 50% every 5 years	80.32	65.76
or	£15,000 annual income increasable by 100% every 5 years	151.44	129.60
Increasing family benefit			
	£15,000 annual income increasing by inflation when paid	192.81	162.84
Decreasing Term			
	(Mortgage protection policy) £30,000 mortgage, 25-year tearm	34.79	24.57

Qualifying policies not only have tax advantages when they pay out, but for policies issued before 14 March 1984 you can also claim a subsidy from the Inland Revenue. The subsidy is worked out at 15% of each premium. You have to be careful not to alter the nature of the policy, since this might affect the tax relief. There is no tax relief for any policies issued after 14 March 1984.

The self-employed can take out special term insurance, called a Section 226A policy, and can usually qualify for tax relief which can cut the cost by up to 60%.

AIDS

If you know you have AIDS, you cannot get life assurance. You would have to disclose the fact to the insurers, and they would decline to insure you. If you knew, but did not disclose it, your life policy would be void. AIDS has not yet had any noticeable effect on premiums for life insurance, but this could change.

Blackstone Franks' verdict

Protecting your dependants from suffering financially if you die is the advantage of term insurance, but the insurance has a set term. This means that if you die after the term, you will not have any cover. These policies are also useful to cover a large inheritance tax bill if death occurs within a certain time. A decreasing term policy will cover the tax due should a donor die within seven years of making a gift.

Unless your policy is to be assigned in connection with a loan, you should consider a form of trust to protect the proceeds from a possible charge to inheritance tax. You should take professional advice to ensure the trust meets your requirements.

Different insurance companies charge different rates. Shop around or use an independent broker.

TRUSTS £££

Trusts are not only for the rich. Even if you are just comfortably off, one type of trust – the accumulation and maintenance trust – can be worth considering for your children, grandchildren or other infants, and many people who are not rich at all set up trusts in their wills. Additionally, you might leave all of your capital in a trust so that on your death the income goes to your spouse, but on your spouse's death the capital is then divided among your children.

You may wish to give a substantial amount of money to your child but do not trust his or her financial wisdom – a trust is a method of dealing with that problem.

Definitions

A *settlor* is the person who sets up the trust and puts money or property into it.

The *trust instrument* is the constitution of the trust which sets out how the trust is to be managed, how the income is to be dealt with, and what will eventually happen to the capital. The instrument is usually either a trust deed or a will which sets up the trust.

The *trustees* are the people who run the trust. They can only run it according to the trust instrument. The settlor may also be a trustee.

The *beneficiaries* are the lucky people who will or may – eventually – be given some money, either as income or as capital from the trust.

A *discretionary trust* is a trust where the trustees can decide who gets the money. The class of beneficiaries may have been decided, eg 'all my children'. A discretionary trust may state that the trustees may pay income or capital in such proportions as they in their absolute discretion shall decide.

A trust with an *interest in possession* is where someone has a right to enjoy the income arising in the trust. For example, if assets are left to Margaret for life, and then her children in equal shares, then Margaret has an interest in possession. The children have what is called a *reversionary interest*, ie they are entitled to the assets when the interest in possession comes to an end (on Margaret's death). Another simple example of an interest in possession is where assets are left to Dennis for 20 years, and then to Carol – in which case Dennis has an interest in possession, but Carol has a reversionary interest.

The person who has an interest in possession is often called a *life tenant*.

The tax consequences

Apart from transfers into an accumulation and maintenance trust, any transfers may be liable to inheritance tax. For gifts out of the trust there is no inheritance tax if it is an accumulation and maintenance trust, but other trusts may have further tax to pay.

Income tax on a discretionary trust, where no one has an interest in possession, is at a total rate of 45% (27% basic rate tax plus 18% additional rate tax). Trusts with an interest in possession, however, normally pay tax at 27% of their income. When trustees pay income to a beneficiary, the beneficiary receives a tax credit of either 45% or 27%. If the beneficiary pays tax at a lower rate, he or she can claim back the difference from the Inland Revenue. If the beneficiary is a higher rate taxpayer, then they will have to pay more tax on receipt of the income from the trust. Trusts are also liable to capital gains tax for gains over £3,300 in a tax year.

Some advantages of trusts

1. It can be an advantage to transfer appreciating assets into a trust to reduce the value of your estate, giving the intended beneficiary

an interest in possession and reversionary interest whereby there will be no further inheritance tax to pay.

2. Trusts are particularly good where you want to reduce the value of your estate without making an outright gift of the assets to someone whose financial acumen is questionable.
3. The accumulation and maintenance trust has a variety of advantages (see next section).
4. As income accumulated within a trust is charged at no more than 45%, it is beneficial for an individual with capital surplus to his requirements and who pays tax at the highest rates to transfer assets to the trust.

Blackstone Franks' verdict
Trusts have a role to play in a variety of circumstances. Before setting up a trust, the capital gains tax and inheritance tax implications must be considered. Remember also that once you have decided to set it up, it is not usually possible to reverse the decision.

TRUSTS - ACCUMULATION AND MAINTENANCE TRUSTS £££

See trusts for a general description.

An *accumulation and maintenance trust* (*A & M*) has several tax advantages, and is commonly used as a way of putting assets into trust for your children while saving tax.

Capital is transferred to the trust. No matter how much capital is transferred, there is no inheritance tax unless the donor dies within seven years. The income made by the trust is accumulated (ie kept in the trust). Any income which is not accumulated must be used for the 'maintenance education or benefit' of the children; school fees, holidays, clothing can be paid by the trust. Assuming the child has no other income, up to £2,425 can be paid without there being any tax charge for each child. If tax has been paid by the trust, then that tax can be reclaimed as a result of paying income to the child.

The trust must come to an end between the child's 18th and 25th birthdays. At that point, the property is shared out. If you do not want the capital to be placed in the hands of the child, you can arrange for the trust to give the child the right to the income instead, while the capital would be given at a later date, eg by the age of 45 or earlier at the discretion of the trustees. You can be a trustee.

If the original capital of the trust is provided by the parents, then any income paid out will count as the parents' income until the child is 18 or married.

The trust is liable to income tax at basic rate (27%) plus the additional rate (18%), ie a total of 45%. Any income paid out for the education or maintenance of the child is treated as the child's income but deemed to be paid after deduction of 45% tax, and may give rise to a tax refund. £1,100 of school fees paid by the trust is regarded as £2,000 of income to the child and if the child's total income is under £2,425 (the personal allowance) then a refund of £900 is due to the child.

There is no inheritance tax when the capital is paid out of the trust to the children. There is no periodic charge to inheritance tax.

Blackstone Franks' verdict

An excellent way for a higher rate taxpayer to create tax-free income for the child. The 1986 Finance Act has allowed unlimited funds to be paid into such a trust without inheritance tax being due, and the trust could include the shares in a family company. In the right circumstances, this can be an excellent device for saving tax and making investments.

U

UMBRELLA FUNDS £££

An umbrella fund is a particular type of offshore fund (*see* separate section). It is a fund operated in a tax haven outside the UK. It is usually managed in the same way as a UK authorised unit trust, but it is not governed by the Department of Trade, nor restricted by some of their tight investment rules. Umbrella funds provide full-time professional management with the share price directly related to the value of the funds managed.

How they work
Some funds operate on an umbrella policy whereby investors can run their own portfolio of investments without any liability to capital gains tax when they switch from one fund to another. The funds usually include a variety of specialist equity funds, bond and money market funds. The equity funds may include Australasia, Canada, Europe, Hong Kong, Japan, Singapore, UK and USA. The bonds may include D-Mark, ECU, Japanese Yen, Sterling, Swiss Franc and US Dollar bonds.

Technically, in an offshore umbrella fund, the investor buys different classes of shares. For example, Henderson's Global Strategy Fund consists of eleven classes: North American shares, European shares, UK growth shares, Japan shares, Pacific shares, Managed international shares, Sterling cash shares, Dollar cash shares, Yen cash shares, Deutschmark cash shares and Swiss Franc cash shares. The share prices are calculated in a virtually identical way to those of an authorised UK unit trust. The major advantage is that the investor can switch from, say, Japan shares to North American shares with no UK capital gains tax liability. This is because the conversion of shares from one class to another does not count as a disposal for tax purposes. The Henderson Fund itself is free of UK capital gains tax and UK income tax. In addition the investor can choose a cash investment (eg Swiss Franc cash shares), which an authorised UK unit trust cannot offer. It is important that the fund maintains a distributor status; the fund managers will ensure that this happens, subject to there being no changes in the UK tax law. The shares are often quoted on a stock exchange (eg Henderson's is quoted on the Luxembourg Stock Exchange).

Blackstone Franks' verdict

Offshore umbrella funds managed by reputable management companies have major tax and investment advantages over authorised unit trusts in the UK. Although there are dangers of losing distributor status, and a lack of Department of Trade controls, with careful selection of fund managers we rank these funds as **£££**. They offer the opportunity to invest in major currencies, and to switch among investments tax free, which the UK unit trust counterpart cannot.

UNIT-LINKED LIFE ASSURANCE ££

Unit-linked life assurance, despite its name, does not have a lot to do with insuring your life. Insurance companies enjoy various tax privileges which enable them to make favourable investments. Unit linking is suitable for both lump sum investors and regular savers. You can buy either an investment bond or a unit-linked savings plan. Both are technically life insurance policies, but usually you only get a small amount of life cover. *See* the section on investment bonds for a full description.

(*See also* unit-linked savings plans and endowment policies.)

Blackstone Franks' verdict

Unit-linked savings plans (endowment policies) and unit-linked investment bonds can be highly successful ways of investing and saving, and can be tax efficient. Consider the investment bond if you are investing a lump sum, and the savings plan if you wish to save over a regular period.

UNIT-LINKED SAVINGS PLANS ££

See endowment policies for full details.

At first glance, unit-linked savings plans may appear to be similar to single premium bonds, but there are differences. The most important one is that with the savings plan you pay a premium at regular intervals (monthly, quarterly or annually), whereas with the single premium bond you only pay the premium once. The unit-linked savings plans can be grouped into three general categories: standard plans, high investment plans, and high life cover plans.

A *high life cover* plan gives you less investment units, and more life insurance. A *high investment plan* gives you little life insurance, but high investment content. A *standard plan* falls between the other two types, with more emphasis on investment, and less on life insurance protection than a high life cover plan.

Blackstone Franks' verdict

You should look on unit-linked savings plans as a long-term

investment. You could get little or nothing back if you only invest for a couple of years. If all you want is life cover, it is unsuitable; see term life insurance instead. If you want the unit trust savings plan, without the life insurance, see the subsection 'unit trust regular savings plans' which is discussed under school fees planning.

UNIT TRUSTS £££

The unit trust is a simple idea. A management company collects sums of money from a large number of people, and with it buys shares in a variety of companies. Each investor holds units in the fund in proportion to the money he or she invests. The notion is that by a large number of people pooling their money they get a spread of professionally managed investments which they would be unable to achieve as individual investors. In addition, unit trusts have a major advantage over the individual investor: the trust is free of tax on any capital gains it makes.

There are two major alternatives to unit trusts: (a) investment bonds, and (b) investment trusts. Read the relevant sections to compare these two with unit trusts.

Over £30 billion is now invested by over three million people in more than 1,000 different unit trusts.

Professional management

Full-time professional expertise should produce better results than the individual can achieve. The administration and paperwork in dealing with share purchases, sales, rights issues, bonus issues, contract notes, etc, are all handled by the managers. They make two kinds of charges. The *initial charge* is included in the difference between the price at which the trust sells units (called the offer price) and the price at which it buys them (the bid price). The initial charge is commonly 5% of the investment. The *annual charge* is normally paid from income earned in the trust, and is usually between 0.75% and 1% per annum. The difference between the offer and the bid price is known as the *spread*.

Pricing

Managers of unit trusts are the only people who can issue units and are obliged to buy back any that an investor wants to sell. Investors can buy or sell units through banks, stockbrokers, FIMBRA members, or direct with the unit trust; the price is usually the same. The managers are strictly controlled by law in the calculation of the prices at which they will buy and sell units, these prices being based on the actual value of the securities and cash in the trust fund, subject to adjustment for charges. The size of the fund can change constantly, as units are created or redeemed to satisfy further cash inflows or repurchases. Prices are quoted in most leading newspapers; both bid and offer prices are shown.

Like any equity investment, prices can go down as well as up. If markets are going down, the professional managers can do little to avoid losses.

Department of Trade and Industry (DTI)

The DTI controls tightly the authorised unit trusts which are freely available to the public. The trust deed governing the management of the unit trust must be approved by the DTI, as must the directors and shareholders of the management company and the trustees. While the managers make day-to-day investment decisions, the trustee holds the cash and securities belonging to the fund to ensure that the managers run the trust in accordance with the trust deed. Trustees are usually major banks or insurance companies. Offshore trusts are not subject to these controls, though they can still be operated by highly respectable managers.

The DTI also makes other rules such as:

1. a unit trust cannot invest more than 7.5% of the trust money in any single company
2. a unit trust usually cannot invest more than 5% of the trust money in unquoted shares
3. it cannot hold more than 10% of a particular class of share in a single company
4. it cannot invest in cash deposits (whatever currency) unless the money is about to be invested
5. it cannot invest directly in commodities or property (but it can invest in shares in commodity or property companies)

There is nothing to stop a unit trust investing in major stock exchanges throughout the world.

Types of unit trust

There are now over 1,000 unit trusts, divided into 18 types, called sectors:

UK General	Middle-of-the-road; up to 25% invested overseas
UK Growth	Capital growth objective; up to 25% invested overseas
UK Equity Income	Income objective; mostly UK
UK Mixed Income	Income objective from mix of equities and fixed rate stocks
Gilt and Fixed Interest Income	Invests in fixed stocks. No longer popular, since direct investment in gilts can give tax-free capital gains, whereas via unit trusts the capital gain is still taxable

Gilt and Fixed Interest Growth	As above
Investment Trust	At least 85% invested in investment trusts (qv)
Financial & Property Shares	85% or more invested in this sector
International Growth	Objective is maximum capital appreciation from range of international shares
International Income	Objective is maximum income from overseas shares, bonds and fixed rate holdings
North American Growth	85% or more invested in US and Canadian companies
European Growth	85% in European stock exchanges
Australian Growth	Capital appreciation objective
Japan Growth	Japanese shares have very low yields, so the aim is growth, not income
Far East Growth	Japan, Australia, Hong Kong, Malaysia and Singapore
Commodities & Energy	Includes gold funds
Managed	Includes trusts which invest in at least four other trusts run by same management group
Exempt	Only exempt if bought by a charity, pension fund, or other funds which are tax exempt

Performance figures

Unit trusts have performed very well on most measures, though with so many of them in the market, some have inevitably done poorly.

A £1,000 investment, with net income reinvested, has done far better than a building society ordinary share account, as shown below:

£1,000 invested	After 5 years £	After 10 years £
Unit trusts (averages)		
European	3,538	8,319
UK General	1,881	5,951
North American	1,106	2,518
Building society	422	1,127

Source: Unit Trust Association. Figures as of 1 January 1987.

But performances can vary in different sectors, and by different unit trust managers, as the following figures reveal:

Returns on £1,000 investment (offer to bid) over one year to 1 January 1987, net income reinvested			
	Best	*Worst*	*Average*
UK General	1,484	1,082	1,188
UK Growth	1,705	929	1,239
UK Equity Income	1,548	1,122	1,253
UK Mixed Income	1,327	1,031	1,195
Gilt & Fixed Interest Growth	1,145	994	1,048
Gilt & Fixed Interest Income	1,162	941	1,031
Investment Trust	1,360	1,078	1,245
Financial & Property	1,396	980	1,230
International Growth	1,702	897	1,244
International Income	1,471	996	1,176
North American Growth	1,265	860	1,049
European Growth	1,654	1,002	1,424
Australian Growth	1,744	794	1,347
Japan Growth	2,047	876	1,589
Far Eastern Growth	2,122	1,238	1,567
Commodities & Energy	1,552	889	1,240

Source: Money Management, February 1987.

Regular saving

Over 50 unit trust managers offer savings schemes in which a minimum of around £20 a month can be invested into a unit trust, bypassing the traditional £500 or even £1,000 minimum lump sum. Unlike endowment policies, there are no penalties for surrendering unit trusts. On the other hand, gains from unit trusts are taxable, whereas if you last out your 7½-year minimum, proceeds from an endowment policy are tax free. This may mean little in terms of practical difference, because your gains on unit trusts are only taxable if you are over the £6,600 annual exemption limit for capital gains.

Tax treatment

The unit trust itself is free from tax on any capital gains. The investor is liable to capital gains tax on any gains beyond his £6,600 annual exemption. Income from a unit trust is liable to income tax.

Regular withdrawals

Individuals with large capital sums available have often favoured investment bonds which give them 5% of their initial investment each year free of tax. A number of unit trust groups operate similar schemes, known as *withdrawal schemes*, in which the trust managers top up the regular distributions of income by the sale of sufficient units to achieve whatever the investor's required level of net income may be. The advantage of such schemes is that the regular encashment of units may be within the investor's annual exempt amount for capital gains tax purposes. The investor may not therefore be restricted to 5% withdrawals. An additional bonus to such schemes is that on death there is no higher rate tax liability (as there is with investment bonds), and any potential capital gains tax on the units is erased.

Selling a family company

On retirement, a family company may sell its assets and goodwill and consist of cash and investments. Such a company could be taken over by a unit trust group which would issue units in exchange for company shares, thus acquiring the portfolio of assets. Normally, the exchange of units for shares would qualify for capital gains tax roll-over relief.

Switching

Selling out of one unit trust fund and buying another is called switching. Because of the bid/offer spreads, switching is expensive. The investor may also be liable for capital gains tax on switching. Many unit trust managers give a discount if you switch among their own group funds. The discounts given are between 2% and 4%, though brokers handling substantial amounts on several clients may negotiate higher discounts.

Blackstone Franks' verdict

Unit trusts are an excellent investment, offering a choice of every sector worldwide, but selecting the wrong unit trust can be expensive. Professional advice is needed to make the right selection. Advisers should be members of FIMBRA or the Stock Exchange.

UNLISTED SECURITIES MARKET £

See also Stock Exchange.

The unlisted securities market (USM) began in 1980 and is a market for shares in companies. Although the USM is referred to as a separate market, it has no real physical distinction. USM shares are traded by stockbrokers just like listed shares, and the price of the shares is quoted in the newspapers. USM companies are 'unlisted' only in the formal sense in that they have not been admitted to full main market listing of the Stock Exchange.

A company might prefer to be on the USM because the entry

requirements are more relaxed, and cheaper, than going for a main board listing. To qualify, the company need only demonstrate a three-year trading record (rather than the traditional five), and even this may be waived at the Stock Exchange's discretion. In addition, instead of a full-scale accountant's report in the prospectus, a USM company can get away with a shortened summary of the financial record. More importantly for the company, the entrepreneur need only sell a minimum of 10% of his company's shares rather than 25% in order to obtain a listing.

Generally, smaller companies - and some weaker ones - have gone on the USM. There have been some spectacular successes, and some spectacular failures. Compared with the main market, the USM has not put up a better performance. The risk/reward scale is much higher on the USM than the main market. The growing, better companies often transfer from the USM to the main market.

Blackstone Franks' verdict

The USM is riskier than a main board listing, but it has not been short of winners.

W

WAR LOAN £££

See Gilts.

WHOLE LIFE ASSURANCE £££

See also life assurance.

Whole life assurance pays out a lump sum when you die – however far in the future. *Without profit* policies guarantee a fixed sum, but because of the higher cost, the without-profit whole life policy is usually not as useful as a renewable, increasable and convertible term assurance contract, unless it is for a special reason, eg to fund eventual inheritance tax. A *with-profits* policy means that the amount which will be paid out increases over the years as the company adds bonuses. This grows like an endowment policy but, unlike an endowment policy, only pays out on death. With some policies you can stop paying the premiums when you reach a certain age (say, 65). You can cash in the policy before you die. A policy may have a guaranteed surrender value. The premiums have to be payable for at least 10 years, and the benefits may be paid out by means of an annuity rather than a lump sum. The policy may often be convertible into another type of life assurance policy such as endowment.

The policy may be on a joint whole life based on two lives (husband and wife, for instance). A joint whole life policy could either pay a sum on the first death, or alternatively pay the sum on the death of the survivor.

A *unit-linked whole life* policy means that your premiums are used to buy units in funds run by the life insurance company. Some of the units are cashed each month to pay for a whole life policy – units left are your investment. With *flexible cover plans* you can choose the amount of life cover you get and therefore how much of your premiums are used for investment, rather than life insurance. You can cash in the policy before you die – but watch out for high surrender charges in the first few years. See unit-linked life assurance.

Because of the improved benefits, whole life assurance is more expensive than term life insurance.

Blackstone Franks' verdict
There are many such policies on the market, and it is easy to choose the wrong type, with the wrong companies. However, a carefully selected policy will protect your dependants from suffering financially if you die, however far in the future. It also enables you to build up a lump sum for your heirs. It can assist in paying an inheritance tax liability on death, especially if a husband and wife leave everything to each other. They could in that case take out a *last survivor* insurance which pays out when the second person dies (ie when the inheritance tax bill is due).

WILLS £££

The consequence of dying without a will can be very serious. Any will made before a marriage, or remarriage, is ineffective – you have to make another one. If you die without a will, there are set rules as to where your estate goes. The advantage of having a will is that your estate will be distributed as you want it to be, the administrators over the estate will be chosen by you, there may not be any unnecessary inheritance tax liability, and the estate is likely to be distributed faster at lower costs.

Professional advice should be taken to ensure that all of the estate is properly disposed of, and partial intestacy is avoided. Careful consideration should be given to what happens if the person to whom you are leaving your estate (eg your wife) dies just before, or at the same time, as you. You should also be aware that a dependant has a right to make a claim against the estate if reasonable financial provision is not made for that person. You may wish to create a trust on your death if, for example, you want the income to go to your spouse, but the capital to go to your children when your spouse dies (*see* trusts).

A new kind of will, called a *discretionary will trust*, enables you to alter your will without going through all of the formalities of drawing up a new will as circumstances alter. This should be carefully discussed with your professional advisers.

Dying without a will
If you die without having made a will, your assets will be distributed according to the rules of intestacy. These rules often lead to an unexpected distribution of your estate. The intestacy rules in England are:

1. *Deceased is married with no children*
   The widow or widower receives:

   (i) All personal possessions
   (ii) First £125,000
   (iii) One half of everything else

The remaining half goes to the deceased's parents. If no parents are alive, the individual's brothers and sisters (or their issue) will share the half-share. If no brothers or sisters or their issue, the widow or widower will take both shares.

2. *Deceased is married with children*
The widow or widower receives:

   (i) All personal possessions
   (ii) First £85,000
   (iii) A life interest in a trust of one half of everything else

   The remaining half passes to the deceased's children in equal shares, who will also inherit the first half when the surviving spouse dies. The surviving spouse may redeem the life interest when all the beneficiaries are adults as the whole estate may then be distributed.

   If the deceased leaves no spouse, but children, the estate is divided among the children equally.

3. *Unmarried, no children*
The entire estate passes to the parents. If no parents are alive, the estate passes to the nearest surviving relatives in the following order:

   (i) Brothers and sisters
   if none: (ii) Children of (i)
   if none: (iii) Grandparents
   if none: (iv) Aunts and uncles
   if none: (v) the Crown

4. *Common law wives*
They have no benefit under the intestacy rules, though anyone dependant on the deceased can make a claim for financial provision under the Inheritance (Provision for Family and Dependants) Act 1975.

A valid will – English law

There are important requirements to meet if a will is to be valid.

1. The will must be signed in front of two witnesses, who also sign.
2. Gifts made to a witness (or spouse of a witness) are invalid, though the will is still valid.
3. A witness cannot be blind, mentally ill, or under 18.
4. Where there is doubt about the mental capacity of the testator, it is advisable that a registered medical practitioner witnesses the will.
5. Any additions or alterations should be initialled by everybody.
6. Nothing should be clipped or stapled to the will.

Blackstone Franks' verdict

You can leave behind much heartache and trouble if you die without a valid will. Make one.

WINE ?

Investing in wine is risky, especially if you invest in wines which are merely passing fashions. The wines must be stored properly, and insured. There are acknowledged good wines, mainly Bordeaux and vintage ports, all of which take some years to mature. There is less risk in investing in such wines, but the rewards are correspondingly less since the increase value is linked primarily to interest rates. Someone has to hold the wines until they are drinkable, whether or not it is an individual, or a wine merchant, and they will expect an appropriate reward for tying up their capital.

Blackstone Franks' verdict
As an investment, illiquid. Purchased for pleasure, highly liquid!

WOODLANDS £

Investment in forestry is highly tax effective. You purchase bare land and plant it (making use of a variety of government grants) and can offset all of the costs of planting the trees (but not the cost of the land) against your other income. Income from the woodlands would normally begin about 25 years after planting, and timber can reach its full maturity at about 75 years after planting. All sales proceeds can be received free of tax – instead, income tax is suffered based on ⅓ of the value of the land when the timber is felled and sold, which is normally a small figure. Woodlands can also be advantageous in the calculation of inheritance tax – large reductions are made for them.

About 9% of the UK is under forest, compared with the EEC norm of 25%. The UK imports about 90% of its timber. Experts anticipate a return of 7% per annum in real terms, which is not very startling for a long-term investment.

Blackstone Franks' verdict
While woodlands are well protected from a tax point of view, this is an illiquid investment, subject to the risks of weather and disease, and depends on timber being of good value in maybe 25 years' time or more. It is a *very* long-term investment.

Z

ZERO COUPON BONDS £

These are fixed interest securities issued by government and large companies, and which carry no dividend. They are accordingly sold at a large discount on their eventual maturity value, thus providing capital growth only. However, under the Finance Act 1984, the capital gain may be liable to income tax.

Blackstone Franks' verdict
Complex tax treatment and not widely marketed. Leave alone. Of interest to UK non-residents sometimes.